Goethe's lyric poems in English transl 1860 • Lucretia Van Tuyl Simmons

Publisher's Note

The book descriptions we ask book-sellers to display prominently warn that this is an historic book with numerous typos, missing text or index and is not illustrated.

We scanned this book using character recognition software that includes an automated spell check. Our software is 99 percent accurate if the book is in good condition. However, we do under-stand that even one percent can be a very annoying number of typos! And sometimes all or part of a page is miss-ing from our copy of a book. Or the pa-per may be so discolored from age that you can no longer read the type. Please accept our sincere apologies.

After we re-typeset and design a book, the page numbers change so the old index and table of contents no longer work. Therefore, we usually re-move them.

Our books sell so few copies that you would have to pay hundreds of dollars to cover the cost of proof reading and fixing the typos, missing text and index. Therefore, whenever possible, we let our customers download a free copy of the original typo-free scanned book. Simply enter the barcode number from the back cover of the paperback in the Free Book form at www.general-books. net. You may also qualify for a free trial membership in our book club to down-load up to four books for free. Simply enter the barcode number from the back cover onto the membership form on the same page. The book club entitles you to select from more than a million books at no additional charge. Simply enter the title or subject onto the search form to find the books.

If you have any questions, could you please be so kind as to consult our Fre-quently Asked Questions page at www. general-books.net/faqs.cfm? You are al-so welcome to contact us there.

General Books LLC™, Memphis, USA, 2012. ISBN: 9781151053213.

❧ ❧ ❧ ❧ ❧ ❧ ❧ ❧

FOREWORD

The present volume is the result of in-vestigations prosecuted during my tenure of one of the Graduate Fellow-ships in German at the University of Wisconsin. My first intention was to supplement and elaborate the investiga-tions already made concerning Goethe's works in English translation, and to give some aesthetic and critical treatment of the individual translations, showing de-fects and virtues, making comparisons, and noting frequent or infrequent mis-understandings of the text. However, the extent of the bibliography soon made it clear that it would take many months merely to copy and compare the various versions which were only to be found in many widely scattered li-braries, and that in the time at my dis-posal I could do little but collate the ma-terial. As a result, the critical estimates have not had the attention which they deserve, but that must be left to a fur-ther publication, now that the ground has been, in a measure, broken, and the material accumulated.

This study is restricted to Goethe's shorter poems and can lay no claims to originality, except that it is the first sys-tematic attempt to collect, under such a title, all of the evidence concerning his shorter poems in English translation. Several investigations of a more general nature have been very thoroughly car-ried out by other students, and I have not hesitated to make the fullest use of their data. A complete list of the books, pamphlets, articles, and manuscripts which afforded me assistance, however slight, will be found in Bibliographies A, B, C, D.

The field of investigation, covering as it did the years from 1790 to 1860, and including anthologies, books, jour-nals, and magazines, soon proved to be enormous. The records were scattered and very inadequate. The fact was re-peatedly emphasized that all of our ear-ly bibliographical data are exceedingly incomplete and inexact, both in this country and in England. No effort has been spared to make my lists accurate and exhaustive, but the contents of many books and anthologies, and par-ticularly of many magazines and jour-nals, could not be completely ascer-tained, since the early ones often had no indices. In spite of searching, page by page, single poems may have been passed over; and again, the data are sometimes uncertain concerning the books themselves, since the early book-lists and catalogues vary among them-selves as to authors, contents, dates of publication, pagination, and volume size. I believe, however, that all the books, anthologies, magazines, or sin-gle translations which had a broad cir-culation or any wide-spread influence in America or in England have been in-cluded here.

I wish to thank, as so many students have done before me, my teacher, Pro-fessor A. R. Hohlfeld, for advice and as-sistance in many ways. His thoughtful suggestions and helpful criticisms have been a constant stimulus and inspira-tion.

The greater part of this work was done at the Library of the University of Wisconsin, which has an unusually large collection of the early magazines of England and America. I wish to take this opportunity to express my warmest appreciation to the librarian, Mr. W. M. Smith, who granted me exceptional privileges, and to the library staff for their great courtesyand valuable assis-tance. Forthe same reasons I wish to thank the librarians of the Boston Public Library, Brown University, the Chicago Public Library, Columbia University, the Congressional Library at Washing-ton, Cornell University, Harvard University, the Newberry Library in Chicago, the New York Public Library, the Osterhout Free Library in

WilkesBarre, Pa., the Pennsylvania State College, Yale University, and the University of Pennsylvania, all of whom readily gave me information, placed books at my disposal and helped me to verify notices which I had obtained. Letters were sent to the librarian of the British Museum and to various English and American publishers, all of whom I would thank for their prompt assistance. To Professor E. C. Parry of Philadelphia, Prof. F. W. C. Lieder, and Mr. Archer Taylor of Harvard University, who gave me important information as to the location of various editions of books, I acknowledge sincerest thanks, and also to Professors F. W. Oswald, F. G. Ruff, and W. E. Roloff, for the use of the material of their dissertations, which are at this time unpublished. These deal with the translations of German literature in English magazines from 1790 to 1880, and it is largely due to them if that part of this investigation is in any way complete. Finally, thanks are due to Professor B. Q. Morgan for a painstaking revision of the manuscript.

Goedekes Grundriss zur Geschichte der deutschen Dichtung (2. Auflage, 1891; 3. Auflage, 1910,) and Eugene Oswald's Bibliography, *Goethe in England and America,* were the starting points of my investigation. However, Goedeke's statements concerning Goethe's poems in English translation depend quite largely upon Oswald's investigations, and Oswald has but twenty entries prior to 1860, so that these two sources proved themselves quite inadequate. Goedeke's work is in general so invaluable that I have tried throughout these pages to make special mention of statements which need rectification. Both of these works would be far more helpful if they gave the year as well as the volume and page of magazines. Then the student would know at a glance whether the reference were an early or a late one.

In some cases almost no data could be obtained. A line of advertisement or a notice of publication in some early magazine or catalog would indicate a book which might possibly be a valuable addition to these lists, but continued

search would fail to find any further trace of the volume. Such cases have been marked with a star in the bibliography. I have tried to reproduce carefully the exact title, and to give the pagination and format wherever obtainable. When possible, the first edition of each book is given, and also the number of editions or reprints, in order to show its circulation and popularity. Often it has required days and weeks of searching in various libraries to establish even such small items. It has not been easy to avoid the occasional repetition of information which seemed to need examination from more points of view and under more headings than one. In a number of cases it has seemed advisable to add brief biographical facts concerning various writers mentioned, since even scant information was not to be found in the various national biographies; the facts here given were taken from the early magazines or prefaces of old publications.

After all the material was at hand, the investigation finally took a two-fold form: first, a full bibliography or list of all literary material which offers translations of Goethe's poems into English prior to 1860; second, a chronological treatment of this material, in order to throw light on the introduction of Goethe as a lyric poet to the English-reading world, and then, incidental to that, to indicate the course of interest and sentiment towards Goethe in England and America. If this study has brought to light any new facts, prepared the way for a more thorough and critical investigation in this field, or shown the need of a truer translation of Goethe's lyrics into English, it will have realized the hopes of its author.

Owing to the late inclusion of some additional items in the bibliographical lists, C and D, the following references need to be corrected.

Page 24, footnote 20, read: Bibliography D, no. 18.

Page 30, footnote 24, read: Bibliography B, footnote 09.

Page 36, footnote 29, read: Bibliography D, no. 41.

Page 36, footnote 30, read: Bibliogra-

phy D, no. 23 and 48.

Page 37, footnote 32, read: Bibliography D, no. 79.

Page 42, footnote 38, read: Bibliography D, no. 48 and 82.

Page 45, footnote 41, read: Bibliography D, no. 61.

Page 46, footnote 42, read: Bibliography D, no. 62.

Page 46, footnote 43, read: Bibliography D, no. 66.

Page 47, footnote 45, read: Bibliography D, no. 47.

Page 48, footnote 46, read: Bibliography D, no. 38,44, 45, 58, 63, 67, 68, 81.

Page 57, footnote 51, read: Bibliography C, footnote 73.

Page 72, footnote 59, read: Bibliography C, footnote 73.

Page 77, footnote 67, read: Bibliography D, no. 73.

Page 90, footnote 74, read: See footnote 48.

Page 90, footnote 75, read: See footnotes 53 and 54.

Page 103, number 82, read: For contents see no. 48.

GOETHE'S LYRIC POEMS IN ENGLISH TRANSLATION PRIOR TO 1860

IMPORTANCE OF TRANSLATIONS

For a long time the question of translations from the Ger"man language into English was left quite uninvestigated. The mediocrity and haste of most of the versions made the whole subject appear to be of secondary importance. Of late years, however, as the importance of comparative literature has been recognized, the value of such knowledge has become more and more apparent. We now realize that whether an author is to be well or ill received, whether his influence is to be broad or narrow, in fact, whether or not he is to be in any degree truthfully understood and appreciated outside of his own country, depends almost entirely upon the spirit and fidelity with which his works are translated. Students interested in Goethe have found here a broad field, the study of which will offer some explanations for the earlier English attitude towards Goethe, and the indifference of the leading literary men of England toward his work. During the latter part of the eighteenth and the early part of the nineteenth century practically all of the knowledge which English readers had of German literature came through translations, since very few of the reading pubilc (not excepting the university men) could read German in the original. Necessarily, then, the tone of English feeling towards German writers was largely dependent upon the quality of the early translations. No small part of the distaste and indifference felt for German literature can be traced to the carelessness, or lack of thorough comprehension, or ignorance of idiom, on the part of the early translators. Very often the meaning was misunderstood or distorted, little was left of the original style, and nothing remained of the original harmony and perfection of phrase. Perhaps no German writer suffered more at the hands of the translators than did Goethe, although it is true that scarcely any author has given the translator a harder task; in the lyric poems especially the difficulties are most evident and the inadequacy of the translations most lamentable.

Goethe himself was among the first to advocate the value of good translations as a step towards better international appreciation, towards a more complete world culture, and towards universal toleration. With this in mind he wrote, in 1828:

Offenbar ist das Bestreben der besten Dichter und ästhetischen Schriftsteller aller Nationen schon seit geraumer Zeit auf das allgemein Menschliche gerichtet. In jedem Besondern, es sei nun historisch, mythologisch, fabelhaft, mehr oder weniger willkiirlich ersonnen, wird man durch Nationalität und Persönlichkeit hin jenes Allgemeine immer mehr durchleuchten und durchscheinen sehen.... Was nun in Dichtungen aller Nationen hierauf hindeutet und hinwirkt, dies ist es, was die iibrigen sich anzueignen haben. Die Besonderheiten einer jeden muss man kennen lernen, um sie ihr zu lassen, um gerade dadurch mit ihr zu verkehren; denn die Eigenheiten einer Nation sind wie ihre Sprache und ihre Miinzsorten: sie erleichtern den Verkehr, ja sie machen ihn

erst vollkommen möglich.

Eine wahrhaft allgemeine Duldung wird am sichersten erreicht, wenn man das Besondere der einzelnen Menschen und Völkerschaften auf sich beruhen lässt, bei der Ueberzeugung jedoch fest hält, dass das wahrhaft Verdienstliche sich dadurch auszeichnet, dass es der ganzen Menschheit angehört. Zu einer solchen Vermittelung und wechselseitigen Anerkennung tragen die Deutschen seit langer Zeit schon bei. Wer die deutsche Sprache versteht und studiert, befindet sich auf dem Markte, wo alle Nationen ihre Waren anbieten, er spielt den Dolmetscher, indem er sich bereichert.

Und so ist jeder Uebersetzer anzusehen, dass er sich als Vermittler dieses allgemein geistigen Handels bemiiht und den Wechseltausch zu befördern sich zum Geschäft macht. Denn was man auch von den Unzulänglichkeiten des Uebersetzens sagen mag, so ist es und bleibt es doch eines der wichtigsten und wiirdigsten Geschäfte in dem allgemeinen Weltverkehr. Der Koran sagt: Gott hat jedem Volke einen Propheten gegeben in seiner eignen Sprache. So ist jeder Uebersetzer ein Prophet in seinem Volke.

1Kunst und Altertum, VI, 1828. or *Goethes Werke, Jubüäums-Ausgabe,* XXXVIII:141.

If we accept this point of view, we can then see the value of a study of the means by which the lyrics and shorter poems of Goethe became known to English readers, of the spirit in which they were translated, of their accessibility in translation, and of the frequency with which these translations appeared. Such a study ought to give a clearer understanding of the poet's position and scope of influence, or lack of it, in the English literary world during the first half of the nineteenth century.

These questions began to receive wider attention with the establishment of the *Goethe-Jdhrbuch* in 1880. In 1882 appeared an article by Prof. Alois Brandl, *Die Aufnahme von Goethes Jugendwerken in England,* and in 1884, a bibliography of translations by Prof. Horatio S. White, *Goethe in Amerika.*

Then followed several bibliographical lists on the subject and finally investigations were made concerning the translations to be found in English and American magazines. These later studies have made possible a specific study of Goethe's shorter poems in English translation and have brought out considerable material not previously obtainable. A glance at the chronological lists of translations (Bibliographies C, D, E) given in connection with these investigations will convey a much clearer idea of the time and attention which was devoted to German translation, and to Goethe in particular, than could be obtained in any other way.

FIRST PERIOD OF THE STUDY OF GOETHE,

1795-1800

It is not necessary to enter into a detailed discussion of the conditions of education and literature in England and America during the period in question. These have been fully treated in the studies previously mentioned. It will perhaps be helpful, however, to mention the various obstacles in the path of the translator in these early years. These were, first of all, the slight social and intellectual contact between the countries, next the difficulty of securing teachers and textbooks, then the almost insuperable difficulty of translating lyric poems faithfully and acceptably, even after the language is mastered, and last and perhaps hardest of all to overcome, the feeling against German taste and literature which dominated England at this time. This has been well stated in a recent study of English poetry:

The influence of the German spirit on the English was far less extensive than that of the French. Few Englishmen in the eighteenth century were masters of the German language, nor was there anything in the social constitution of Germany which could furnish to the English aristocracy models of taste and manners at all approaching the standard of refinement presented by the French court. In the more popular paths of English literature, German examples operated mainly by intensifying the character of the Romantic revival. German literature was swarming with spirits and spectres, castles and convents, tales of marvel, magic, and mystery. From Germany the taste for the supernatural, returning with added force to England, found expression in the fictions of Mrs. Radcliffe and "Monk" Lewis, and in the numerous imitations of Burger's famous ballad, "Lenore".

Following this trend of literary taste towards the supernatural and the mysterious, it was this same "Monk" Lewis who

Courthope, W. J., *History of English Poetry,* VI:20, Macmillan, 1910.

'Matthew Gregory Lewis, called "Monk" Lewis, was born in London in 1775, and died at sea while returning from the West Indies, in 1818. He was educated at Oxford and studied German at Weimar in 1792 and first introduced some of Goethe's ballads into England. Hereafter for a few years German literature began to assume a new, interesting, and impressive character in English eyes. One critic spoke of the many German dramas on the English stage and said, "It is a time when our novels are German, our poetry German, and nothing but German is admired." Lewis's romantic novel, *The Monk,* which was published in London in 1795, and which gave him his name henceforth, inaugurated an epoch in English literature. It was interspersed with German ballads, all exemplifying some demoniacal, elemental power; among these was Goethe's *Erlking,* which immediately became popular. This version of the *Erlking* was further circulated by publication in the *London Monthly Mirror* for 1796 and the *Philadelphia Weekly Magazine* for 1798. It appeared again in Lewis's *Tales of Wonder* (1801), with his version of *The Fisher* and Walter Scott's paraphrase of *Der untreue Knabe,* called by him *Frederick and Alice.* "

At about the same time that Lewis was studying German in Weimar, Walter Scott was taking up the study in Edinburgh. He had been led to it by his admiration for translations of some of Burger's ballads, and continued his reading for some years. In 1797 he saw

Lewis's translation of *The* 1793, where he met Goethe personally. Upon his return to England, he tried to make known to his countrymen that sort of German literature which had appealed to him. His much censured novel, *The Monk,* appeared in 1795 and contained numerous translations from the German. In 1798 he met Walter Scott and influenced him to continue his study of German and to attempt translation into English. He procured the publication of Scott's translation of Goethe's *Obtz* and later asked him to assist in the production of his *Tales of Wonder,* 1801, and *Tales of Terror,* 1807. During the rest of his life, Lewis translated many dramas and romantic tales from German into English.

London Monthly Mirror, V: 355, 1798. This is rather a paraphrase than a translation, for the original poem of Goethe, which appeared in 1776 in *Claudine von Villa Bella,* has six stanzas of seven lines each, while this version has twenty-two stanzas of four lines each. For further discussions of Scott's work as a German translator see Brandt, *Die Aufnahme von Goethes Jugendwerken* in England, in *OoetheJahrbuch,* 111: 27, 1882: Blumenhagen, K., *Sir Walter Scott als Ueberseteer,* Rostock, 1900; Elze, K., *Sir Walter Scott,* Dresden, 1864; Hohlfeld, A. R., *Scott als Uebersetzer* (Studien z. vgl. Lit. Gesch., 111:498); Lockhart, *Life of Walter Scott. Erlking* and was tempted to try a translation for himself. This he sent to Lewis for criticism, and their friendship dated from that time. Scott's version was not made public at the time of translation but appeared among his collected works in 1806. In 1798 he made the version of *Der untreue Knabe* which Lewis used in *The Tales of Wonder. Gbtz* was translated in 1799 and also *Der Klaffgesang der edlen Frauen des Asan Aga.* This last poem has never been included among his collected works, but was printed, together with the *Erlking* and *Frederick and Alice,* under the title, *Apology for Tales of Wonder,* and privately circulated. Scott had the poet's appreciation for a great poet and felt deeply the beauties of the great German

artist (whom he always called Goethe). However, he was not willing to study thoroughly, and had no opportunity to learn, by hearing, the finer shades of meaning and the adaptation of words to moods, as used in Goethe's poems; thus his translations are not exact either as to content or as to the mental picture which they produce. No doubt the work which he did helped to stimulate interest in other Englishmen, but it cannot be said that he gave any great impetus to the growth of public liking for Goethe. His translations, like all of these early ones, served only to introduce Goethe as the author of weird and uncanny ballads, without in any way revealing him as a talented lyric poet.

In Germany many of Goethe's shorter poems had become popular as songs and had been variously set to music. In the same way, some of the shorter poems became known in England about 1798.

This was largely due to a certain Mr. Beresford, whose Scott's *Erlking* has the following interesting heading, "To be read by a candle particularly long in the snuff. The Erlking is a goblin that haunts the Black Forest of Thuringia. " This version was also found in the *Philadelphia Portfolio,* 1808, IV:32.

"*Neue Lieder* in Melodien gesetzt von Bemhard Theodor Breitkopf. Leipzig, 1770. *Yolks-und andere Lieder mil Begleitung des Fortepiano* in Musik gesetzt von S. Freiherrn von Seckendorff, Weimar, 1779, Dessau, 1782.

It has been difficult to get definite knowledge concerning this man and his name. The reviews in the magazines of that time refer to him simply as Mr. Beresford. The *Encyclopedia Britannica* does not mention him. Prof. Brandl, in the *Goethe-Jahrbuch,* 1882, III: 71, speaks of work in translating seems to have been considerable but has been hard to trace definitely. He is first mentioned on the title page of a book which appeared in London and Berlin in 1798: "*German Erato* A collection of favorite songs translated into English with original music. The translator is the author of Specimens of German Lyrics, Mr. Beresford.'' This allows us to assume the existence of a collection of German lyrics translated by him into English prior to 1798. Thus far, however, no record of this first volume has been found, either in the book lists of the time or in the magazine reviews. The *German Erato* contained the following of Goethe's poems: *Mignon, The Violet, The Harper's Song, The Fisher,* and *To the Moon,* all with musical accompaniment by Reichardt. In 1798 appeared, likewise in Berlin and London, *The German Songster"* with Reichardt's duet music, containing these same poems, "by the author of German Erato". In 1800 and 1801 there was issued inLondon,in royal octavo, a sort of magazine entitled, "The German Museum or Monthly Repository of the Literature of Germany, the North, and the Continent in General, with numerous sheets of music by Mozart, Reichardt, and Weisse". It contained some of the above poems in Beresford's translation, and added to these a trans him as, "Rev. J. Beresford, Englischlehrer der jungen KiJnlgln von Freussen." The *London Dictionary of National Biography* names a certain Rev. J. Beresford, who took his degree at Oxford in 1798, who was a rector and wrote some religious books, but no mention is made of any German translations or collections of lyrics nor of any residence abroad as tutor to the Queen of Prussia, a fact which would scarcely have been omitted. A long obituary notice of this same man. Rev. J. Beresford, in the London *Gentlemen's Mag..* 1841, XV:548, is likewise silent as to these facts. I believe rather that the translator is Rev. BenJ. Beresford. Allibones' *Diet, of Authors* mentions Benjamin Beresford as the translator of poetical pieces from the German, with the original music, in 1797. (This may be the original edition of his lyrics). Furthermore, the *London Poetical Register* for 1804 and 1805 has several songs translated from the German by B. Beresford, also the *London Monthly Review,* 1805, XLVIII:75, contains an article on the life of Kotzebue. "translated from the German by Rev. Benj. Beresford, English lecturer to the Queen of Prussia." It may be possible that the two are identical,

but I am led to believe not. and that the correct name is BenJ. Beresford rather than James, as several authorities give it.

"See Bibliography *D,* no. 2.

"See Bibliography D, no. 3. "See Bibliography *D,* no. 5. lation of Goethe's *Mahomet.* Further search shows that these versions were almost the only ones circulated in the British and American magazines and journals for nearly twenty years, that they were welcomed with praise, and that frequent reference was made to them. Very few further attempts were made to translate any of Goethe's lyrics for two decades. Here and there a stray poem or two is to be found in the magazines or in some ponderous collection, but there was no decided increase. In 1821, Beresford's translations appeared again, this time with the following title page: *Specimens of the German Lyric Poets Translated into Verse, from Burger, Goethe, Klopstock, and Schiller.* No name was given as author, but the preface stated:

The chief portion of the following translations was published at Berlin about twenty years ago in a musical work comprising some of the best German melodies. The words to those melodies were from the pen of an English gentleman of the name of Beresford, who was long a resident in Germany. They met with so favorable a reception that the same publisher was afterwards induced to print them without music in two volumes. The great popularity which they obtained, their scarcity and unquestionable merit, are the motives which gave rise to the present reprint.

A few more poems translated by Mr. Mellish, British consul at Hamburg, have been added. The one copy of this "See Bibliography *D,* no. 9.

"Joseph Charles Mellish (1768-1823) is not mentioned in the *Encyclopedia Britannica* or in the *Dictionary of National Biography.* A few interesting facts concerning him were found in the *Proceedings* of the Manchester Goethe Society for 1888, and also in the *American Monthly Magazine and Critical Review,* 1819, 4:293. About 1795 he married and settled in Weimar; later

Schiller bought his house and made it his home. Mellish enjoyed the friendship of Schiller and Goethe, his son was Goethe's god-child and there is a poem of Goethe's, written in 1818, *An Freund Mellish.* He tried to overcome the influence of Kotzebue in England by translating *Wallenstein* and *Maria Stuart.* He translated each act of this latter drama as soon as it was finished by Schiller, so that the English version appeared before the German. In 1798 he translated Goethe's *Hermann and Dorothea,* in 1801, *Paleophron and Neoterpe,* and contributed to Wieland's *Merkur;* in 1802 he became British consul to the Hanseatic Cities and went to reside at Hamburg. While here, in 1819, he published a volume of original poems in the German language and added a few German translations, but none from Goethe. He died in Hamburg in 1823.

book obtainable in this country was found at Harvard University. It was dated "1822, second edition", but press notices were found which stated that it was in circulation in 1821. It went through another edition in 1823 and still another in 1828.

Since this, so far as concerns Goethe's poems, is evidently the same collection of translations as appeared in 1798 and 1800, since it is the first collection of Goethe's verse to be received in England, and above all, since it was the first effort to introduce Goethe as a poet of something more than bizarre ballads, it deserves more than passing mention. The translations from Goethe are largely if not entirely the work of Beresford; they fill pages 31 to 40 of the 152 pages in the volume. They include: *Moonlight (An den Mond), The King of Thule, The Fisher, The Harper, The Violet, Mignon,* and *The Hunter's Evening Lay.* The translations show a thorough knowledge of the language, but they do not reproduce the simplicity and directness of the original poems. The style seems stilted. The attempt to translate, to shape into rhyme, and moreover to make the English meter fit the German melodies, which were composed for the original poems—all this was more than the skill of the translators could do, and more than the evanescent charm of the poems could endure. They are all rather sweetly pretty and artificial, they never ring true with genuine emotion, and they all suffer from the stilted verbosity of that age.

The tranquil words of Goethe, in *To the Moon*

Fullest wieder Busch und Thai
Still mit Nebelglanz,
Losest endlich auch einmal
Melne Seele ganz;

become transformed into:

Scattered o'er the starry pole
Glimmers Cynthia's beam,
Whispers to the softened soul
Fancy's varied dream.

Nearly all of the other stanzas are similarly elaborated. *The Violet,* which is so simple and pathetic in Goethe's words, becomes here nothing but commonplace:

Unnoticed in the lonely mead
A violet reared its modest head,
A sweet and lovely flower!
A blooming maid came gadding by
With vacant heart and gladsome eye,
And tripped with sportive careless tread.

The Fisher has lost all of its original character and gives us now more of a humorous impression than anything else:

In gurgling eddies rolled the tide;
The wily angler sat
Its verdant wlllowed bank beside
And spread the treacherous bate.
Reclined he sat in careless mood
The floating quill he eyed,
When rising from the opening flood
A humid maid he spied.

And the end of the fourth stanza expatiates thus:

Tempts thee not yon aetherial space
Betinged with liquid blue?
Nor tempts thee there thy pictured face
To bathe in worlds of dew?

The translation of Mignon is the most successful of all the collection; in it the translator has kept the original tone, rhyme, and rhythm rather closely:

Know'st thou the land where citrons scent the gale,
Where glows the orange in the golden vale;

Where softer breezes fan the azure skies,
Where myrtles spring and prouder laurels rise?
Know'st thou the land?
'Tis there our footsteps tend;
And there, my faithful love, our course shall end.

Know'st thou the pile, the colonnade sustains,
Its splendid chambers and its rich domains,
Where breathing statues stand in bright array
And seem, "What ails thee, hapless maid?" to say?
Know'st thou the land?
'Tis there our footsteps tend;
And there, my gentle guide, our course shall end.

Know'st thou the mount, where clouds obscure the day,
Where scarce the mule can trace his misty way,
Where lurks the dragon and her scaly brood.
And broken rocks oppose the headlong flood'
Know'st thou the land?
'Tis there our course shall end;
There lies our way, ah, thither let us tend.

Over thirty different versions of this poem were found, printed in the years from 1798 to 1860 and of all of them this one of Beresford stands among the best. To one who reads the original it shows faults, but on the whole it succeeds well in giving the original spirit. In this regard it is much better than Carlyle's translation (1824 in *WUJielm Meister)* which has been most widely reprinted and is the version most generally known to English readers. His is a translation of words but not of moods, and runs thus:

Know'st thou the land, where lemon trees do bloom,
And oranges like gold in leafy gloom;
A gentle wind from deep-blue heaven blows,
The myrtle thick and high the laurel grows?
Know'st thou it then?
'Tis there, 'tis there,

O, my beloved one, I with thee would go!
Know'st thou the house, its porch with pillars tall?
The rooms do glitter, glitters bright the hall,
And marble statutes stand and look me on;
"What's this, poor child, to thee they've done?"
Know'st thou it then?
'Tis there, 'tis there,
O, my protector, I with thee would go.
Know'st thou the mountain bridge that hangs on cloud?
The mules In mist grope o'er the torrent loud,
In caves lie coiled the dragon's ancient brood,
The crag leaps down and over it the flood:
Know'st thou it then?
'Tis there, 'tis there,
Our way runs, Oh, my father, wilt thou go?

Another early version appeared in 1817, in the *North American Review,* IV: 201, and purported "to be done by a celebrated English bard" (unidentified). I give this because it is a fair example of the distortion of many of the other efforts, and shows so clearly how little mere words can translate a poem of Goethe:

Know'st thou the land where stately laurels bloom,
Where orange groves exhale their rich perfume,
Soft breezes float along the lucid sky,
And all is peace and joy and harmony?
Know'st thou the land?
O, thither flee,
And dwell forever there, my friend, with me.

The three stanzas of the original are not enough, and this writer adds a fourth, wherein he urges us to

Spurn the vile herd, indignant fly

To some more courteous land and milder sky.

With these early attempts of Lewis, Scott, and Beresford, the first period of German study in England closed, partly due to the fact that public taste for ballads of terror and tales of wildness had waned, but more largely due to the political reaction against foreign influences. The excesses of the French Revolution and the ambitions of Napoleon had produced a revulsion of feeling against all things revolutionary. Since Goethe, as the author of *Werther* and of *Gotz,* was known as the head of the "Storm and Stress" movement for individual freedom, all attempts to make him better known were for a time fruitless. Up to the year 1800, we may say, the English world had very little reason to think of Goethe as a distinguished lyric poet. Very little of that side of his genius had reached England and what had come was decidedly inadequate. Judging from these translations alone, and not knowing the orignal poems, the English reader could scarcely feel that in their author there was any surge of great genius.

LACK OF INTEREST FOR ABOUT TWENTY YEARS 1800-1820

The political reaction against continental ideas lasted until about 1820 or 1822, and was reflected in English views of literature. During these years, whatever attention the critics and essayists gave to Goethe was directed to *Faust, Wilhelm Meister, DicTituwg und Wahrheit,* and *Die Wahlverwandtschaften,* rather than to the shorter poems. The longer works received during this interval at least twenty-five reviews, varying from one to fifty-four pages in length, whereas in the same period scarcely twenty-five single translations of Goethe's lyric poems are to be found. Even Beresford's collection was not reprinted until 1821. In America much the same condition prevailed, since magazines and books were largely reprints from England. If anything, the interest here was still slighter. Only twelve reviews of Goethe appeared in American magazines during these two decades, and about the same number of single poems in translation.

One review of fifty-four pages, which appeared in 1814 in the *London Quarterly Review* (X:388), and also in the *Neiv York Quarterly Review* (X:355), shows clearly the general tone of literary criticism just at this time and some-

thing of the attitude towards Goethe's lyrics:

Goethe's smaller poems, numerous as the sands of the sea, we have neither time nor inclination to criticise in detail. Most of them have some sort of whimsical originality, many have considerable pathos, and all are more or less immoral. The marvelous is, with him, a very favorite source of effect, and his extensive reading has enabled him to draw largely not only on the superstition of the middle ages, but on those of the classical and oriental paganism. The fancies of the German peasants furnished him with the Erlking, the tale of The Student in Magic and his wooden water-bearer is circumstantially taken from the Philopseudes of Lucian, as is the Spectre Bride of Corinth from the story of Philinnium and Machates, quoted in many old demonologies from Phlegon Trallianus de Mirabilibus et Longevis. Few of these deserve translation and even if they deserved it better, translations would be impossible. where the greater part of the charm consists in a boundless command of the German language and an authority still more extraordinary over every species of rhythm of which that language is susceptible. Werter, his earliest romance in prose, the delightful pastoral of Hermann and Dorothea, the marvelous dramatic poem of Faustus, are sufficient indeed of themselves to serve as a foundation of no common fame, and it is by these and these alone, in our opinion, that his renown is to be extended in foreign countries or prolonged to any remote continuance in his own.

This review shows us that even during this period interest, study, and appreciation were not entirely stagnant. I quote rather extensively from these early reviews, because I believe that they give us, at first hand, the thought of the leading literary men of the day, and that they show us the ideas which were being disseminated among the reading public.

It was during this period of lack of interest that Mme. de Stael's book, *De L'Allemagne,* appeared. It had a large influence both in England and America

in maintaining and stimulating an interest in Goethe and in helping to draw attention to his lyrics. Her book did not attempt to translate many of the shorter poems, but it did emphasize their perfection and help to bring the lyric genius of Goethe into proper perspective. The book appeared in English translation first in London, 1813, and the next year in America; it went through several editions, was widely circulated, greatly discussed, and extensively reviewed. Twenty-one long reviews were found in English magazines and five in American magazines. These reviews indicate that a change was occurring in the attitude of literary England toward Goethe; when a freer intercourse again opens up between the two countries, it will no longer be the young poet of youthful passion and exaggeration who will be studied, but the calmer, philosophic man of letters. Such a one as has been revealed to them through the autobiography, *Dichtung und Wahrheit,* through Schlegel's lectures, which were being regularly translated

"*Germany,* by the Baroness Stael-Holsteln, translated from the French. London. Murray. S vols. 1813; New York, Eastburn, Kirk do. 2 vols. 1814; Boston, Houghton, Mifflin Co. 1 vol. 1859. (Part I, chap. 15, deals with Goethe and Weimar; part II, chap. 7, deals with Goethe, also chapters 21, 22, 23.) into English, and through Mme. de Stael's book. Very often these reviews resolved themselves into criticisms of Goethe and his works in particular, as was the case of an article published just at the end of this period in the *Scot's Magazine* for 1820 (VI:331), entitled *Remarks on the Miscellaneous Poetry of Goethe after reading Mme. de Stael.* This shows quite a different point of view from the preceding criticism, and manifests an interest in a number of lyrics which heretofore had been entirely ignored by English students and readers. The critic sings the poet's praise thus:

Goethe's lesser pieces, which make up what is called his miscellaneous poetry, are in almost every instance so finely and even philosophically conceived, that they may be regarded as poetical exhibitions of the most valuable remarks which a scientific student of human nature could choose to see made. The genius of this author is of such a nature that a trivial subject seems sometimes to have had charms for him, from the consciousness which he felt of his power of investing it with unusual attractions. It is the talent of Goethe to view with interest every variety of human creatures. Among his miscellaneous poems are several exquisite pieces of a lyrical character and in a strain almost peculiar to Germany. Among these may be classed Song of Mahomet, To my Goddess, A Journey to the Hartz during Winter, and The Wanderer. In these the author has carried forward a fine but distinct allegory In such a way that the most common understanding can follow his meaning, while at the same time the thought is possessed of an elevation and richness that fit it for conveying delight to the most accomplished mind.

From this it appears that slowly but surely a juster estimate was forming, and there were other indications, in the magazines of both countries, that a desire was growing for a fuller understanding of Goethe. More people were trying to study and read German in the original, more textbooks, leaders, and dictionaries in German were published and advertised, and more and more young men were going to Germany to study.

Just one man in the literary world during these earlier decades seems to have gone systematically to work to have German literature truly recognized and comprehended in England. He must be acknowledged to be the first one who really effectually introduced the modern poetry and drama of Germany to English readers. This was William Taylor of Norwich, who began his work in 1790, and in various ways kept it before the public for forty years, until it was summarized in 1830, in his *Survey of German Poetry,* in three good sized volumes. This book was the first general view of German literature to be printed in England, as it was the first to give any attention to the body of Goethe's shorter poems as a valuable contribution to the world's literature. As such it deserves a notable place in the history of German literature as related to German thought. Taylor's personal point of view in criticising German life and thought was often narrow and provincial, his knowledge of German idiom was sometimes at fault, he did not by any means recognize the true greatness of Goethe, nor did he grant him his proper position in the literary world. His attitude was one of intolerance toward Goethe's whole career as a man, but he did much to draw attention to the lyric poems as a noteworthy part of Goethe's accomplishment. When the book appeared, Carlyle subjected it to very harsh criticism, saying that it was not literary, not historical, and not in any way a portraiture of the national mind of Germany. As we now view it from a greater distance, we are inclined to think that it did not merit the comdemnation which it received at that time. Carlyle did however recognize the intrinsic merit of the work as an index to the general change in mental at See Bibliography *D, no.* 16. William Taylor of Norwich (17651836) was well educated, travelled considerably, and visited Weimar in 1782. He devoted himself to literary and journalistic work, and was well known in his day as the contributor of many articles to the leading magazines, such as the *Monthly Review, Monthly Magazine, Annual Rev., Critical Rev.,* and *London Atheneaum.* It is said that he contributed, in all, one thousand seven hundred and fifty articles to the various magazines, mostly criticisms of foreign literature and largely attempts to bring about a better appreciation of the German poets. For a fuller discussion of William Taylor and his work, see Robberds, J. W., *Memoirs of William Taylor of Norwich,* 2 vols. Murray. L. 1843; also an article in Manchester Goethe Society *Proceedings* for 1890; and William *Taylor of Norwich,* by Georg Herzfeld, in *Studien zur engl. Philologie,* vol. II, 1897.

litude towards German literature which was gradually coming about in England, as the following quotation shows:

"Within the last ten years independent readers of German have multiplied perhaps a hundred fold, so that now this acquirement is almost expected as a national item in liberal education. Hence in a great number of minds, some immediate personal insight into the deeper significance of German Intellect and Art;—everywhere at least a feeling that it has some significance. We regard this renewal of our intercourse with poetic Germany, after twenty years of languor or suspension, as among the most remarkable and even promising features of our recent intellectual history. Does not the existence of such a book betoken that a new era in the spiritual intercourse of Europe is approaching, that instead of isolated, mutually repulsive National Literatures, a World Literature may one day be looked for? The better minds of all countries, by whom ultimately all countries in all their proceedings are governed, begin to understand each other, to love each other, and to help each other.

A large part of this important book of Taylor's is made up of lengthy translations from the German. In discussing Goethe's poems, he gives Beresford's version (without acknowledgment) of *The King of Thule, Mignon's Song,* and *The Harper,* and his own translation of *The Fisher, The Spirit's Greeting, The ErlMng, The Song of Mahomet, The Wanderer, The Bride of Corinth* and *The Apprentice to Magic.* Taylor's translations are done with care and are generally faithful to the main ideas of the originals, they are at least readable without being ludicrous and they give a reflection of the original dignity and worth of Goethe's lyrics. In general they lack lightness, and they do not show a broad command of rhyme and rhythm, but taken with those of Beresford they give the fairest, truest view of Goethe's work that had yet reached England.

In *The Apprentice to Magic* he has been most successful, and has kept most truly the rhythm and structure of the original. His version reads smoothly, but the English construction is often far from natural, as the first stanza shows clearly: - *Edinburgh Revieiv*, XXXV: 153, 1831, also to be found in vol. Ill of Carlyle's *Essays.*

Now that my old master wizard
Is for once at least away,
All the spirits in his keeping
Must my sovereign will obey.
Watched have I his word and deed
Many an hour and many a day,
And with strength of mind and head
Work a wonder, I too may—
Wander, wander,
Yonder, yonder,
To the brook along the path.
Bring me water,
As you taught are,
Pour it, shower it,
In the bath!

The Song of Mahomet is least successful in reproducing for the foreign reader any of the real tone of Goethe's poem, in which the short and flowing lines have every syllable packed with significance. The English language seems almost inadequate to render the German and becomes heavy and awkward in the reproduction of these lines. One stanza will show the difficulties which Taylor encountered and also his lack of clear comprehension of the meaning of the original:

Seht den Felsenquell,
Freudehell,
Wie iSternenblick;
Ueber Wolken
Nahrten seine Jugend
Oute Geister
Zwischen Klippen im Gebusch.
Jiingling frisch
Tanzt er aus der Wolke
Auf die Marmorfelsen nieder,
Jauchzet wieder
Nach dem Himmel.

See where the rocky spring, clear, bright, as joy,
Bursts from amid the bush-encircled cliffs;
Like to a glittering star
Between the streaks of cloud,
Fresh as a youth he hastens from his bed
And dances gladly on the marble floor,
And backward springs with glee
To the eye of Heaven.

This book was one of the last efforts of the old literary spirit. A new school with new views and conceptions now took up the work in a larger, broader manner. It was no longer the youthful Goethe of the Storm and Stress period, the writer of weird ballads, the poet prodigy, who shocked authority by his *Gotz,* and society by his *Werther,* that the English students were now eager for, but it was the man Goethe, viewed from all sides of his genius.

SECOND PERIOD OF THE STUDY OF GOETHE, 1820-1860

This period of fuller and truer comprehension was greatly forwarded by the warm enthusiasm of Thomas Carlyle, whose championship, beginning about 1822 in the various British magazines, lasted many years. He gave his point of view in one sentence in his introduction to the translation of *WiChelm Meister,* in 1824. "Minds like Goethe's are the common property of all nations, and for many reasons all should have a correct impression of them.'' This was his belief and this was the line along which he worked in all his criticisms and essays. He felt that there was a strong intellectual current in Germany which imperatively demanded attention, and he determined that the English public should learn its value. He therefore set himself busily to work to give his fellow countrymen information, to remove as far as lay in his power their prejudices, and by means of translations to supply them with the means of understanding his praise. Not only did he offer them knowledge, as Taylor had done, but he hammered it in by a long series of essays and articles in the various magazines, such as *The Edinburgh Review, The Foreign Review, The Foreign Quarterly Review, Fraser's Mag., New Monthly Mag.,* and *Westminster Review.* He made many references to Goethe's shorter poems, but the most direct statement of his estimate is found in a paragraph of his introduction to the translation of Goethe's *Tales,* in the volume called *German Romance* (1827):

Of his numerous short poems it is difficult to say a well-weighed word; for they are of all sorts, grave and gay, descriptive, lyrical.

"For a discussion of Carlyle's studies in German and of their influence on him, see Roe, F. W., *Carlyle as a Critic of Literature,* Columbia Univ. Press, 1910; Boyesen, H. H., *Goethe and Carlyle* in *Essays on German Literature,* Scribner, 1898; *Critical and Miscellaneous Essays of Thomas Carlyle,* edited by Ralph W. Emerson. Munroe Co. Boston, 1888; *Carlyle's Essays,* vols. I. II, III, as published in his collected works.

didactic, idyllic, epigrammatic, and of all these species, the common name, without long expositions, would, when applied to him, excite a false idea. Goethe is nowhere more original, more fascinating, more indescribable, than in his smaller poems. One quality which very generally marks them, particularly those of a later date, is their peculiar expressiveness, their fulness of meaning. A single thing is said and a thousand things are indicated. They are spells which cling to our memory, and by which we summon beautiful spirits from the vasty deeps of thought. In his songs, he recalls to us those of Shakespeare: they are not speeches but musical tones; the sentiment is not stated in logical sequence, but poured forth in fitful and fantastic suggestions; they are wild wood-notes of the nightingale, they are to be sung not said.

Carlyle did not attempt to translate any of these shorter poems, except the songs of Mignon, Philine, and the Harper as they occur in *Wilhelm Meister.* These, it is evident, he worked over with loving care and understanding, but he was no poet, and he could not sink his own personality, so there is more of Carlyle than of Goethe in the results. The gentle, mournful words of Mignon, whom he calls "the daughter of enthusiasm, rapture, passion, and despair, whose history runs like a thread of gold through the tissue of the narrative", have been too ephemeral to be caught by him, as has been shown in a previous quotation. On the other hand, the ballad of the Harper, as translated by Carlyle, is strong and ringing, and may be accounted one of the best of all the translations which have been made:

"What notes are those, without the wall,

Across the portal sounding?
Let's have the music in our hall
Back from its roof resounding."
So spoke the king, the henchman flies,

His answer heard, the monarch cries,
"Bring in that ancient minstrel."

Yet even here there is a ruggedness that does not exist in the original. Another version, which appeared in the *Edin* "These same poems were translated by Boylan, R. D., In a second translated version of *Wilhelm Meister,* in 1855, for the Bohn Library, where they have found broad circulation. But they are by no means so poetical or true as Carlyle's.

burgh Literary Journal (vol. I, 1829) and was circulated at the same time as Carlyle's, will show the superiority of Carlyle's rendering, and at the same time emphasize the difference in effect produced by a poor choice of synonyms: "What minstrel voice is that that rings

So blithely by my castle wall?
Command the joyous wight that sings
To appear within and bless my hall."
The king commands, the page forth flies,

The page returns, the monarch cries—
"Admit, admit the old man to me,
. That makes my court resound with glee."

Carlyle's insistent arguments and efforts were slowly bringing results and a truer estimate seemed apparent in the tone of all literary reviews of the period. In 1828, the following criticism appeared anonymously in the *London Weekly Review* and was reprinted in the *Museum of Foreign Literature and Science,* in Philadelphia and New York, thus reaching many readers:

The lyric is the most original and fertile of all the poetic sources. In order to form a just estimate of the poetry of a nation, we must be well acquainted with its lyric writers. To us it appears surprising that our translators from the German should not have employed their exertions on this point instead of pan-

dering to a vitiated taste by presenting only tales of ghosts, goblins, robbers, and boisterous knights, or the still more contemptible scenes of maudlin sentimentalism with which they have been pleased to afflict the public. Few attempts have been made to introduce the German lyrics among us and those few have not afforded any real information on this very interesting portion of German literature. Goethe's smaller pieces contain some of the most original conceptions of modern poetry, uniting as they do the simplicity of the Greek with the depth of the German, and perfectly free from that besetting A criticism and review in connection with the edition of *Qoethes Werke* in 40 volumes by Cotta, Tubingen, 1827-1830. It contained anonymous translations of *Abschied, Ntihe dee Geliebten, An die Entfernte, Schflfers Klagelied, An den Mond,* and *Wandrers Nachtlied.*

So far as I have been able to ascertain, Goethe's collected works, printed in German, were first published in London, in 1833. in 10 vols., by Schloss. See *London Athenaeum,* p. 585, 1833. In English, they were begun in 1847 by the Bohn Library. See Bibliography *B,* footnote 68.

sin of our times, a straining after effect by florid diction and forced display. The author's principal power in these smaller poems arises from his fine perception of nature, not like Wordsworth attaching himself to vulgarities, but perceiving and calling forth beauties in objects unnoticed by the ordinary observer. He is the Raphael of poetry, whose chaste delineations are for all people and for all times. Goethe's smaller poems, flowing, ingenuous, and elegant in thought and expression have become, as it were, the national property of Germany, resounding alike in the palace and the peasant's humble dwelling. It is the child of nature, breathing the universal language of the human heart.

No greater praise nor fuller appreciation than this has been forthcoming even in the poet's native land, or in these later decades when the opportunities for fuller knowledge and freer judgment are at hand.

The next earnest attempt to translate Goethe's lyrics for English readers, an attempt in line with the endeavors of Carlyle, was made by Charles Des Voeux, a young man who had lived and studied in Weimar. His book was published in London in 1827, and revised and reprinted in Weimar in 1833. It was called *Torquato Tasso, a Dramatic Poem from tJie German and other German Poetry,* and included eighteen shorter poems of Goethe, quite the largest collection which had yet reached England. The title page says that the book was given out, "with the approving kindness and encouragement of Goethe", and the author's desire was, as stated in his preface, "To give a specimen of that simplicity and feeling which may be considered peculiarly characteristic of German poetry". That was exactly the attitude to be desired, but the book does not seem to have achieved its purpose. The author has remained comparatively true to the thought and the form, but in trying to retain the rhyme and the meter he has lost the very simplic

For contents see Bibliography *D, no.* 13. Further details concerning Des Voeux may be found in the *Proceedings* of the English Goethe Society, London, 1891, 6:134.

See Goethe's letters to Zelter of March 28, 1827 and to Carlyle of January 1, 1828; both of which go to show that Goethe appreciated the attempt but was not quite certain of the literary value of Des Voeux's work. ity which he aimed to reproduce. This volume was reviewed in several of the leading magazines of the day, but I could not find that it had an enthusiastic reception by its readers, or that the versions were reprinted in any of the magazines or anthologies of that period. Goethe may have given his approval to these translations because he thought of Des Voeux as one more "Vermittler des geistigen Handels" between England and Germany, and not because he found any marked superiority in the translations themselves. Des Voeux was the first to translate for English readers *The Shepherd's Lament, Consolation in Tears,*

Wanderer's Night Lay, To the Chosen One, Night Thoughts, and *Welcome and Farewell.* One stanza from *Mignon's Song* and his version of the *Wanderer's Night Lay* will serve to show clearly the lack of simplicity and directness which kept this collection from being a good reflection of the original:

Know'st thou the land, where fair the citron blows?
And with dark leaf the golden orange glows?
From the blue heaven soft breathing gales descend.
The myrtle still, the laurel scorns to bend.
Know'st thou It well?
Oh there, oh there,
Might I with thee, my truly loved, repair!

Wanderer's Night Lay finds expression in these lines:

Thou who from Heaven above art sent.
Thou who every sorrow stillest,
Him who with twofold pangs is rent
With a twofold life thou flllest.
By passion's strife I'm tossed and torn
As joy and woe exchange their part,
Oh leave me not, Sweet Peace, forlorn.
But come, oh, come into my heart.

The finest of all his efforts is his translation of *To the Moon,* which is far truer than Beresford's and yet leaves much to bo desired:

Again thou flllest brake and dell
With dim and misty glance,
Again my soul avows thy spell
And melts in liquid trance.
Thou sheddest thy all soothing beam
O'er this thy chosen spot,
As Friendship's eye with mellowed gleam
Illumes my destined lot.

These early translators failed to see that there was in Goethe a natural clearness of mind which made him scorn anything like a trick or conventionalism in style, and which led him to avoid all obscurity and commonness of expression. Yet these are just the points where they failed, Des Voeux among the rest. Thus we cannot say that his efforts had much effect in bringing about any better appreciation of Goethe's lyrics.

The broader attitude towards Goethe, which Carlyle was furthering and Des Voeux wished to foster, was much assisted by the writings and translations of Mrs. Sarah Austin, who had been one of the circle of young literary workers about William Taylor of Norwich. She wrote with a devotion to the subject, an understanding, and a tolerance which could not do otherwise than carry conviction. She lauded Goethe as a lyric poet and illustrated her praise by a number of the shorter poems in her own translations: *Prometheus, Vanitas,* one *Elegy (Manche Tone sind mir Verdruss), Wanderer's Night Song, Mieding's Death, EupJirosyne, Lili's Park,* and *Metamorphosis of Plants.* Her book came out in 1833, in three volumes, called *The Characteristics of Goethe, from the German of Folk, von Mutter and Others;* it was widely circulated and very thoroughly reviewed. Her presentation of Goethe and his work and life, as well as her translations, gave glimpses of Goethe from a new, uncommon, and more personal point of view. After reading the reviews in the magazines, it is plainly evident that she did much to broaden the estimate of English and American readers. Since none of the poems which she included in her book had previously been printed in English, they formed quite an addition to English knowledge and helped to lessen English prejudice.

See Bibliography *D,* no. 19, for contents and full list of literary reviews. The *Dublin Univ. Mag.* (VII: 1, 1836) says of this work, "It is the most valuable work on German literature ever put in English."

Considered as translations, they are careful, accurate, and fluent, but like so many of the translated versions they lack lyrical fire. There is a lifelessness about the poems which makes us feel that they are words and not the burning expression of a great soul.

It can be said for the early pioneers in this field that thfy did change the point of view of the English world towards the poet Goethe, but not that they were able to present his lyric poems adequately.

THE WORK DONE BY THE BRITISH AND AMERICAN MAGAZINES

Prom this time on, much of the knowledge of Goethe's lyrics came through the magazines, and comparatively little was given out in separate book form except for the occasional anthology. Recent investigations in the earlier magazine literature have revealed much interesting material, and have shown that the magazines acted as the advance guard in this gradual invasion of England by the knowledge of German literature. They did not merely reflect public taste, they rather shaped and directed it. Considering the large number of native interests, political, religious, social, literary, with which British magazines could have busied themselves at this time, it is astonishing to see how much time, space, and acute criticism they devoted to things German and to Goethe in particular. First came the reviews of *Werther* in 1779, then followed reviews of the early dramas, then of *Faust,* and later of the prose works. *The Edinburgh Magazine,* founded in 1790, the *London Monthly Mirror* (1798), the *London Monthly Magazine* (1798), the *Edinburgh Review* (1802), the *Quarterly Review* (1809), all printed frequent comments, reviews, and single poems. They represent the early efforts of the circles of Lewis, Scott, Taylor, and their friends. Goethe's name and fame could have remained unknown in very few corners of the reading world. It was a magazine article on *Faust,* in the *New Edinburgh Review* of 1822, which introduced Carlyle as a champion of Goethe. More and more space was given to criticisms of Goethe and to transalations of his poetry. However, prior to 1830, *Blackwood's Magazine* was the only journal which had con " See Bibliography *A:* Davis, B. Z., *Translations of German Poetry* in *American Magazines 1H1-1810;* Goodnight, S. H., *German Lit. in Amer. Mag. prior to 1846;* Haertel, M. H., *German Lit. in Amer. Mag. 1816-1880;* Oswald, F. W., *German Lit. in Eng. Mag. 1810-1835;* Roloff, W. E. , *German Lit. in Eng. Mag. 18S5-1860;* Wilkins, F. H., *Early Influence of German Lit. in America.* sistently continued its articles on German literature. Through the work of its editor, Lock-hart, and the broad and intelligent discussions of R. P. Gillies in the series of articles called *Horae Germanicae* in its pages, from 1818 to 1824, it had a broad influence in dispelling English ignorance and prejudice. In 1844 and 1845, it printed a long series of translated poems of Goethe. This was the work of W. E. Aytoun and Sir Theodore Martin, and was the largest and most representative collection of the poems which had yet appeared in England as well as by far the best translations theretofore made. These appeared in book form in 1859 and will be discussed later among the individual volumes of poems. In 1846 *Blackwood's Magazine* printed translations of some of Goethe's poems "After the antique manner", and in 1856 in an anonymous article, *Wayside Songs,* several other poems, heretofore untranslated, were added to the list. Thus their readers had a fuller idea of the breadth and range of Goethe's short poems than any other readers could have had at that time in England.

A series of very excellent translations from the German poets began to appear in 1835 in the *Dublin University Magazine* and continued until 1846, under various titles, *Anthologia Germanica, Stray Leaflets from the German Oak,* and *Lays of Many Lands.* Nearly all were unsigned but were the work of a gifted young Irish poet, James Clarence Mangan. These translations were collected in two volumes, called *A German Anthology,* in 1845, and printed in Dublin, then reprinted in New York in 1859. They will be more fully discussed under the head of anthologies. When Mangan ceased to contribute to the *Dublin University Magazine* in 1849, Sir Thepdore Martin took up the work and published a number of translations under the pen-name of "Bon Gaultier".
See Bibliography *D,* no. 40; *Blackwood's Magazine* 1819, IV; 1820, VII; 1823, XIII; 1824, XV, XVI. Also Bibliography C, no. 3. See Bibliography *D,* no. 23 and 47, *DubHn Univ. Mag.* 1835. V; 1836, VII; 1837, IX. *Dublin Univ. Mag.*

1849, XXXIII:609. *A Bouquet of Ballads* contains *To his Mistress, With a Ribbon, May Song, Love's Dream, Love in Absence.*
The *London Athenaeum,* from the time of its first issue in 1828, gave much attention to German translations and particularly to Goethe and his work, but it never emphasized his worth as a lyric poet. The same was true of *Fraser's Magazine,* founded in 1830; numerous single poems translated by various writers and many reviews and criticisms are to be found in the following years, but generally they are desultory and unemphatic in character. However, in 1859, one very thoughtful and critical article, written by Arthur Hugh Clough, appeared in this magazine. It dealt with Goethe as a lyric poet and insisted on a close and more careful translation of his poems; it was reprinted in the *Eclectic Magazine* in Boston, and thus had a wide influence. One extract from this will serve to show the broadened view and truer attitude which the literary men were taking towards Goethe's lyrics and towards the translation of them:

In translating a great poem like the Iliad or any great work of any great writer like Goethe, the really important thing is to give the peculiar, individual, and distinctive character, and perhaps yet more than elsewhere is this the case where the poems are brief and lyrical, where the story is little and the style much. Goethe's lyrics will not be worth a great deal, if they are not presented in a style and manner nearly approaching that style and manner in which Goethe wrote them and expressed himself. We have the portraiture of a particular human mind to re-portray, and the fine personal details of a human experience to re-express. Some delicate autobiographical confidence is perverted by every seemingly slight alteration; some spiritual communication is re-communicated amiss; the scientific values of some subtile and exact psychology are, in the new notation, falsely conveyed. And there are bits of his verse where the outlines are as hard to copy as those of antique sculpture. Were we asked to name the compositions which above all

others bring before us the man Goethe, and place us in communication with his mind and spirit, we should turn to such poems as Prometheus, Mahomet's Song, The Limits of Humanity, The Song of the Spirits over the Waters, and Ganymede. These may well serve for the English reader to show the point of view from which the great German writer regarded the world and the things of the world, visible and invisible, sensual and supersensual.

"See Bibliography *D,* no. 77. *Goethe's Poems and Ballads,* in *Fraser's Mag.* LIX; 710; *Eclectic Mag.* XLV:560.

In America during the first decades of the nineteenth century, as has been said, knowledge, opinions, and taste were formed according to the English standards, and all reviews and criticisms were largely reprints from the English magazines, but gradually, as American national life became separated from the English, American thought and opinion began also to take a different trend. About 1820 the spirit of literary independence began to pervade the American magazines. Carlyle's essays and translations, Madame de Stael's and Mrs. Austin's books were widely circulated and independently reviewed. What Carlyle was trying to do in England, Emerson and his friends, Channing and Margaret Fuller, assisted by Bancroft, Motley, and Ticknor, were trying to do in America, but they were carrying their studies of Goethe even further. It was the spiritual and philosophical side of Goethe's work in which these thinkers were interested, and even among his shorter poems it was that quality which they sought. There was a large circle of New England Unitarians who took active part in making the literature of Germany, particularly Goethe, known to the American public. The list of these men, who were at one time or another Unitarian ministers, shows the close contact of American Unitarianism and German letters at this time: C. T. Brooks, S. G. Bulfinch, J. F. Clarke, J. S. Dwight, N. L. Frothingham, W. H. Furness, E. E. Hale, F. H. Hedge, Theodore Parker, George Ripley, John

"Weiss, all of whom gave considerable attention to the works of Goethe and nearly all of whom translated some of his poems. As a result we find the Americans introducing the more abstract poems in preference to the simpler songs and ballads. In this work, the *North American Review* of Boston and New York, *The Christian Examiner* of Boston, *The Western Messenger* of Cincinnati and Louisville, *The Dial* of Boston (edited by Margaret Fuller), *The Southern Literary Messenger* of Richmond, *The Democratic Review* of Washington and New York, and *The American Monthly Magazine* of New York and Boston, took the lead. This list shows that the interest

"Braune, P. A., *Margaret Fuller and Goethe,* Holt & Co., 1910.

was by no means confined to New England, although it probably centered there. In 1824, in *The North American Review,* George Bancroft printed a long criticism of Goethe's worth as a poet, *The Life and Genius of Goethe,* and gave his own very creditable translation of nine of the short poems, in this way antedating any lengthy article in the English journals. In 1836, in the *Western Messenger,* James F. Clarke explained the situation clearly:

A few years ago the name of Goethe was hardly known in England and America, except as the author of a silly book, Werther, an incomprehensible drama, Faust, and a tedious novel, Meister. So at least our critics called them. But now a revolution has taken place. Hardly a review or magazine appears that has not something in it about Goethe, and people begin to find with amazement that a genius as original as Shakespeare and as widely influential as Voltaire has been among us.

Owing to the puritanic traditions of American students, we find many long tirades against Goethe and his views of art and life as subversive of good morals, but nevertheless they studied him, they learned from him, and they were broadened by him. It was Goethe's balanced genius and philosopliy of life which they wished to understand, and they found it expressed even in the

shorter poems and epigrams. Consequently we find the following translations from American pens, which were not found at all in England until Bowring's complete collection appeared in 1853: *Stability in Change, Song of the Spirits over the Waters, My Goddess, The Divine, The Harz Trip in Winter, Eagle and Dove, Ganymede, The Limits of Humanity, Proemium, Epirrhema, Orphic Sayings, Proverbs,* and *Epigrams in Rhyme.* Thus the American magazines may be considered as a leading agency in making known the shorter poems of Goethe to the American reading world, and in broadening the conception of his genius as a lyric writer. The greatest obstacle which they had to struggle against, and which they never succeeded in overcoming, was the objection to his so-called "immoral principles". Professor Goodnight, in summing up See Bibliography D, no. 10. *North Amer. Rev.,* 1824, XIX:303.

the general work of the American magazines from 1800 to 1846, says:

It is clear that no great change in attitude took place in regard to Goethe. At the same time, the lists show him to have been by far the best known of the German writers. Perhaps a gradual change did take place in the country at large, a change wrought more by the poems and dramas as they became known, than by the criticisms. Notwithstanding the acrimony of some critics, and although the objectionable phases of Goethe's life and works were never wholly lost sight of, it seems not unreasonable to suppose that, from 1833 to 1846, at least, the public had for him "an always ascending regard."

And Professor Haertel, speaking for the period from 1846 to 1853, says:

Goethe is made more prominent than any other author. He is highly esteemed as an artist, and the question as to his life and morals is falling into the background, although by no means forgotten. His genius is almost universally recognized and lauded, but his philosophy is still looked on askance.

Goodnight, S. H., *German Literature in American Magazines prior to 1846,* p.

91, Bulletin of the University of Wisconsin, 1907.

"Haertel, M. H., *German Literature in American Magazines,* 1S461S80, p. 19, Bulletin of the University of Wisconsin, 1908.

WORK DONE BY THE POETICAL ANTHOLOGIES

Another agency which was strong at this time in spreading the knowledge of Goethe's poems was the poetical anthology. Many reasons combined to make anthologies popular. Few people owned or cared to buy entire sets of any one author's works, but seemingly every one wanted a few selections from each author. As soon as literary intercourse between Germany and England revived and the German poets began to be recognized, translations from German writers were included in these anthologies. During the years from 1800 to 1860 scores of anthologies were published; over sixty were found which presented translations from the poems of Goethe, and many more were examined which did not include him. After 1828, scarcely a year passed without adding several anthologies which included Goethe's poems to the list, and the years from 1840 to I860 were especially fruitful. Some of these were of little literary value and were short lived; they are mentioned in the printers' lists of the time, but further than that no trace is to be found of them. A very few were important and lived through several editions, and these will be mentioned in detail. Most of them contained only a small number of poems by any one author, and were evidently compiled from the translations most easily accessible, with no thought of their quality and with no idea of demonstrating the range or variety of the individual authors represented in their pages. The selections of the poems of Goethe in nearly all of the anthologies is strikingly similar: *The Harper, Mignon, The Violet, The Heather Rose, The Fisher, The Erlking, The King of Thule, New Love—New Life, Bliss of Tears, Nearness of the Beloved, To the Moon,* were seldom omitted. Only in a few cases do the translated versions of the German poems rise above mediocrity, since they are neither careful in workmanship nor especially successful in reproducing the lyric mood. Even with three or four of the best of these collections at hand, and the assistance of the frequent versions in the magazines, it would have been difficult for the inquiring student of Goethe to gain any adequate idea of his shorter poems. The anthologies helped to extend the general knowledge, but they did little to increase a truer appreciation of Goethe as a poet.

Among the early books of this sort we have already mentioned Des Voeux's *Tasso and Other German Poetry* (1827), which offered eighteen selections from Goethe's poems. Another of a similar nature was *The Song of the Bell and Other German Poetry,* by J. J. Campbell, in 1836. This contained fifteen poems from Goethe, among which there were new: *Wont and Done, Drink Song, Ergo Bibamus, Artist's Song,* and the *Prolog to Faust.* The thought and the spirit of the original poems seems to have been a secondary consideration; so hard did the translator strive for clever rhymes that even his English sentences were distorted, and very little of the original impulse of the German poem was left. This lack of ease and of vitality may be shown in the following lines from *Wont and Done:*

I have been in love, but first aright,

Once was I the servant, but now the slave quite,

Once was I the servant of all!

This essence of charms has made captive of me,

She does what I want or for love or for fee,

All others but she on me pall.

None of the anthologies of the following years have any particular merit or novelty, nor do they emphasize Goethe's work as a lyricist. No convincing note was struck until 1845, when the versions of J. C. Mangan, which had previously been made for the magazines, were collected and published under the name *German Anthology,* in two volumes. It

"See Bibliography *D,* no. 25, for full contents.

"See Bibliography *D,* no. 47 and 80. James Clarence Mangan was born in Dublin in 1803 and died there of the plague in 1849. His edu cation was broad and included Latin, Spanish, French, and Italian. He studied German thoroughly in order to read German philosophy. Very early in life he began to write original verse and was soon recognized as a genius, but he never achieved success because of his intemperate was first published in Dublin and later, in 1859, through the efforts of a few warm friends it was reprinted in New York, and again in 1884 in Dublin. However, the collection seems never to have found the broad circulation which its merits "warranted. That Mangan had a true appreciation of the great task which lay before him, when he tried to present Goethe to his English readers, is shown by his own words in an article appended to some of his translations in the magazine:

Goethe probably wrote more for an undeveloped future than for his own era. Throughout his works we frequently stumble upon skeletons of thoughts whose gigantic and foreign aspect startles us, "but which, we have no doubt, hands competent to the task will hereafter fill up with the flesh and blood essentials of vitality. It forms indeed the great glory of this wonderful man that his obscurity rarely strikes us as being other than veiled luminousness.

To this true sense of value he added splendid poetic talent, a fine command of language, a facility in rhyming and a keen sense for melody. The reviews and criticisms which his anthology received show that he stood high in the esteem of his contemporaries. One of them states very clearly a quality which is at once noticeable in his translations and which has been largely lacking in his predecessors:

Mr. Mangan's mind is precisely of that plastic character which Is indispensable for spirited and truthful translating. He possesses in a high degree the art of thoroughly divesting himself, in his capacity of translator, of every individuality of thought and manner, and of becoming, so to speak, the mere instru-

ment of the author whom he translates, so that the thought, the words, the form, the style, the manner, are faithfully rendered back.

habits. He was generally In distress and led a secluded life. Most of his work was published either anonymously or under the pseudonym of "Clarence". Beside original verse, his entire literary work was given to translations. From the German he included translations from Goethe, Schiller, Herder, Klopstock, Richter. Gellert, Salis, Mathisson, Heine, Hslty, Nicolal. Kerner, TJhland, Tieck, Fouque, Freiligrath, Simrock, Burger, Rlickert, Chamlsso, Arndt, and many minor writers. *"Dublin Univ. Mag.,* VII:301. 1836. *"Dublin Review,* XIX: 312, 1845.

After a thorough study of his translations, we can scarcely give them such unqualified praise, although they do take very high rank. His virtues are his weakness, for his unbounded command of his own language, his freedom in verse, and his fondness for quaint expressions sometimes led him to deviate and to adorn the lines which he was translating. Nevertheless, we find here for the first time a ringing, swinging quality in the lines, they sound genuine, they echo in one's memory, and they have lost to a large extent that stilted and superficial tone which has been so evident in most of the previous versions, as a few extracts will show: From *Hassan Aga:*

What white form is shimmering on yon lea?

Is it snow or is it swans we see?

Snow? It would have melted in the ray.

Swans? Long since they must have flown away.

Snow it is not, swans it cannot he;

Tis the tent of Hassan Aga shining.

There the wounded warrior lieth pining,

Mother, sisters, all to tend him come,

But his wife, too shame-faced, weeps at home.

or from *The Minstrel:*

"What voice, what harp, are those we hear

Beyond the gate in chorus?

Go, page, the lay delights our ear,
We'll have it sung before us."
So spake the king: the stripling
flies—
He soon returns: his master cries,
"Bring in the hoary minstrel!" or
from the *Song from the Coptic:*
Quarrels have long been in vogue
among sages,
Still though in many things wranglers
and rancorous,
All the philosopher-scribes of all ages
Join in a voice, on one point to anchor
us.
Here is the gist of their mystified pages,
Here is the wisdom we purchase with
gold;
Children of light, leave the world to its
mulishness,
Things to their natures and fools to their
foolishness.
Berries were bitter in forests of old!
Mangan's susceptibility to mood, fa-
cility in rhyme and originality of ex-
pression are strikingly shown in *The
Treasure Seeker:*
Sick at heart and lank in purse,
I dragged my snake-like days along,
Want is man's reproach and curse
And Gold is bliss—thus ran my song.
So, to end my woes and pains,
A treasure crock I went to roll up:
Stuck the sharp steel in my veins
And signed the bond that gave my
soul up!
Other translations of his that are excellent are *The Fisher, The Violet, The
King of Thule,* and *The Lay of the Captive Count.* Very few of Mangan's
translations have been included in any
of the general anthologies or later eclectic volumes of Goethe's poems which
have come within the bounds of this investigation, and yet he did more than
any translator, up to his day, to show to
the foreign reader the ease, versatility,
and melody of Goethe's verse.

The next book of translated verse
which offered any considerable number
of Goethe's poems was *Metrical Translations from the German* by "A German
Lady" (Mrs. Adela Haller). This collection included twenty-five poems from
Goethe, nearly all taken from his early
lyrics, (as given under the title "Lᵈeder"

in Goethe's collected works). The author made these translations with great
care, evidently, and from pure love of
the task, hoping thereby to show to her
English friends something of the beauty
of her own German poets. However, she
had not the necessary command of English rhyme and meter, and her grammat-
ical constructions are so distorted in her
effort to fill out the verse forms, that
there is little ease and grace in the lines.
The result is highly unnatural composition, as shown for instance in the lines
To a Golden Heart:
Thou remembrance of enjoyments
flown,
Still worn near my heart,
Still uniting those whose souls would
part,
"See Bibliography *D,* no. 59.
Would'st thou lengthen Love's short
days, now gone?
Lilly, can I fly thee? To thy chain
Bound, through foreign land
Through far vales and woods my way I
wend.
Lilly's heart not soon from mine again
Could be disengaged;
Like the bird once caged.
Of all these anthologies, the one
which gained the largest circulation was
The Poetry of Germany by Alfred
Baskerville. It was published in London, Leipzig, New York, and Philadelphia, and had gone through fourteen
editions up to 1886. It is to be found
in nearly every reference library in the
country, and as a reference book it has
the advantage that the German text is
printed on one page and the English
translation on the opposite page. Twenty-three of the best known of Goethe's
poems are given, in versions tolerably
faithful to the text, but devoid of poetic
spirit. The selection shows that
Goethe's poems included a very broad
range of subjects, and the book might be
valuable as assistance to those who are
trying to work out a translation from the
German, but the renderings themselves
are the merest doggerel.

One other anthology was rather widely circulated at this time: *Specimens of
the Choicest Lyrical Productions of the
Most Celebrated German Poets from*

Klopstock to the Present Time, by Mary
Anne Burt. It was first published in
Leipzig in 1854, and then re-edited in
London in 1856. This book gave biographies and literary notices on each author, and worked out the translations
with care and exactitude, as far as ver-
bal content was concerned. The selection from Goethe's poems was slightly
different from the preceding anthologies, in that to the first seventeen songs
(as given in Goethe's collected poems)
and to a few of the well-known ballads a
translation of the *First Walpurgis Night*
was added. Here the same judgment
must be given as in the preceding case:
the versions are prosy and mechanical,
and there is nothing in them which
would mark their author as a poet of
eminence. I have not been able to find
that any of See Bibliography D, no. 60.
"See Bibliography *D,* no. B4.
the translations of Baskerville or Burt
have ever been reprinted or quoted in
any other collections of verse.

A few other anthologies followed
those already mentioned in England, but
none had any great variation in the selection of poems, none had any distinction for excellence of translation, none
were widely reviewed, nor had any of
them an extensive circulation.

In America, as well as in England, the
anthology of poetry seems to have been
very popular. Previous to 1842, English anthologies alone were current in
America and were often reprinted there,
but after that time anthologies compiled
by American authors, and containing
translations made by them, began to appear thick and fast. Like the English
ones, very few of these have been able
to hold a lasting place as literature.

So far as can be ascertained, the first
anthology which was not a reprint of
an English publication was *The German
Wreath* by Hermann Bokum, in 1836.
Most of the translations from Goethe in
this book were not original, but were
taken from the Beresford-Mellish collection of 1821 and from Taylor's *Historic Survey* of 1830. The book, which
offered nine of Goethe's poems, had not
a large circulation, but was used rather
as a reader for students of German at

Harvard College. After this beginning, various collections of verse were published in different parts of the country, but none of them laid stress upon Goethe's work and none of them contained more than three or four of his poems.

In the same year (1845) that England received from Mangan its best anthology, America also received its best and most representative anthology; this was Longfellow's *Poets and Poetry of Europe,* published in Philadelphia and London. It was very well received and favorably reviewed in both countries, and has maintained its place down to the present as one of the best books of its kind. In presenting See Bibliography *D,* no. 24. Hermann Bokum was a German by birth and was one of the first instructors of German at Harvard College.

"See Bibliography *D,* no. 46. Higginson, T. W., in his *Life of Longfellow,* (p. 189), says of this book. "It is intrinsically one of the most attractive of a very unattractive class".

the poems of Goethe, the editor did not give his own work, but exercised much care and thought in order to select what he considered the best translations which had yet been made. Since Longfellow was not only well versed in German literature, but also possessed much poetic talent and appreciation, his choice is interesting. His list included the *Dedication of Faust* by Fitz-Greene Halleck, the Cathedral scene in *Faust* by A. Hayward, *May Day Night* by Shelley, *Salutation of a Spirit* by Bancroft, and the following poems by J. S. Dwight: *Solace in Tears, Loved One Ever Near, To the Moon, Vanitas, Mahomet's Song, Prometheus,* and *Song of the Spirits over the Water.* The only work of his own which Longfellow included was the translation of the two *Wanderer's Night Sortigs.* Here we find, for the first time in an anthology, some of the "Oden in freien Rhythmen", and we are struck by the broad variety of types of poems selected, although in this variety not one ballad is present. Here we begin to notice that same difference in the selection of poems which was evident in the magazine literature

of America, and in a number of the American compilations of verse, edited from 1845 to 1860, by Bancroft, Everett, Furness, Hedge, Frothingham, Margaret Fuller, and J. S. Dwight. It is interesting to note that all of these writers, like most of the New England circle, had been influenced in their general attitude towards Goethe by their reading of Madame de Stael's *Germany.* None of their compilations, however, gave any considerable space to Goethe's shorter poems. In none of the books, except those by Margaret Fuller and by Dwight, was Goethe's lyric talent emphasized. It was Goethe the disciple of individuality, culture and freedom of spirit, whom they studied, and it was that side of his writings which they stressed. With Goethe as a poet pure and simple they were not concerned, and their translations generally show that it was the thought rather than the beauty of form and style which they tried to reproduce.

Summing up the work done by magazines and anthologies during the period under discussion, it may be said that from

"See Bibliography *D,* No. 37, 43, 44, 57, 61, 65, 66, 79.

1820 to 1840 these agencies brought a widening knowledge of Goethe's lyrics, but showed no remarkable fineness in the quality of translation. Theirs was a work of dissemination. Prom 1840 to 1860, there was manifested a truer appreciation of Goethe and a juster estimate of his poems, also the quality of translation was higher. However, it could not be said that through these agencies alone any broad conception of Goethe as a lyric poet was made possible. It was the appearance of single volumes of Goethe's collected verse which began to accomplish what the magazines and anthologies had undertaken.

INDIVIDUAL VOLUMES OF GOETHE'S COLLECTED POEMS

It is rather remarkable that whereas the other works of Goethe were translated frequently and very quickly after their publication in Germany, the collected poems were not attempted for many years. As has been shown in the pre-

ceding pages, almost every side of Goethe's genius was recognized and could be studied and fairly well estimated from the English translations, but no thorough knowledge of him as a lyric poet could be obtained by any who did not read German in the original. There seems to have been no attempt, and no suggestion even, to make a translation of the collected poems of Goethe. The relatively few poems which appeared in the magazines and anthologies represented but a small part of Goethe's varied range in poetry. In the main, only the very early songs, the ballads, and a few of the later lyrics had been translated and circulated broadly, as a glance at the bibliography, list E, will show. The ballads were the greatest favorites: *Mignon,* 47 translations; *The Erlking,* 47; *The Fisher,* 44; *The Minstrel,* 29; *The King of Thule,* 25 (exclusive of the versions in the 18 translations of *Faust* prior to 1860); *The Violet,* 20; *The Captive Count,* 19; *The Apprentice in Magic,* 17. Among the other poems we find the numbers somewhat smaller: *Nearness of the Beloved,* 26; *Prolog in Heaven,* 25; *Heather Rose,* 16; *To the Moon,* 16; *Spirit's Greeting,* 15; *Vanitas,* 14; *Wanderer's Night Song,* 12; *Prometheus,* 12.

The first volume which brought a large number of Goethe's poems together, and which really tried to show the variety of his lyric genius, was the one arranged by John S. Dwight, published in Boston in 1839 and called *Select Minor Poems Translated from the German of Goethe and Schiller.* "See Bibliography C, no. 1. *Select Minor Poems of Goethe and Schiller,* John S. Dwight, 1839. Hilliard, Gray, & Co. Boston, vol. Ill ol *Specimens of Foreign Standard Literature,* edited by George Ripley.

An examination of this volume shows that it was the compiler's wish to present Goethe as a poet striving for the highest culture, not as an eccentric sentimentalist or as a writer of startling ballads. The broad view which Dwight took is well stated in his introduction:

The lighter lyric pieces are the most genuine things the poet does; into them goes most of the character and nature of the man; in them you have him under all his moods and aspects; and if they win you to their mood and haunt you long, you feel that you know him. Could Goethe and Schiller he brought near us in some such living way, it would give a new impulse to our literature, and inspire worthier aims and methods of culture than now prevail. The living movement, which commenced with them, tells us how life and thought and poetry and beauty are the inheritance of Man and not of any class or nation; and how each, however humble, by fidelity to himself shall find the natural current of his own being leading back into the very bosom of that ocean.

As to method, he says:

The versions have been made upon the principle that the spirit and the form are inseparable in all true poetry. In every piece, with only two or three exceptions, the measure and the rhyme have been exactly preserved and the thoughts rendered very nearly line for line. Of course they fall far short of what could be desired. The peculiar genius and capabilities of every language are, and always will be, an obstacle to any perfect translation.

This collection is by no means complete, as it contains only eighty-five of Goethe's shorter poems, but it serves to show better than any previous collection the many-sidedness of Goethe's lyric genius. Dwight's selection makes the volume unique for its period: of the early songs and lyrics there are included thirty-six; ballads, eleven; miscellaneous poems, sixteen; Art, four; God, Soul, and World, ten; and a few selections from the parables, epigrams, proverbs, and Orphic sayings. Most of the translations are the work of Dwight himself, to which he added seventeen translations made by other Goethe students of that time: George Bancroft, James F. Clarke, William H. Channing, Margaret Fuller, F. H. Hedge, N. L. Frothingham, and G. W. Haven; thus this book really represents the scholarship and appreciation of the new literary generation, which had been inspired by German university training, and which

was trying now to share the enjoyment of lofty verse with those who could not study it as they had done. Many of the poems that had previously seemed indispensable in any collection are missing in this one, but on the other hand many are here rendered for the first time into English: *Stability in Change, Proemium, World Soul, Harz Journey in Winter, Ganymede, Limits of Humanity, The Divine, The Youth and the Millstream, Trusty Eckart, Artist's Evening Song, Cupid as Landscape Painter, For Life (Die glucklichen Gatten), On the Lake, Prophecies of Bakis, Tame Xenia, Proverbs, Epigrams.* This book was very widely and favorably reviewed in this country, and found a ready reception. In England, in spite of its broader scope and novelty in selection, it seems to have been little known. Its author never sought to spread it by securing an English publisher, as many American writers then did. I have found only one review of it in any of the British periodicals, and that was in 1844, in the *Dublin University Magazine,* which had been printing Mangan's translations and was just about to publish his *Anthology of German Verse.* It granted that the authors understood their originals, but it feared that a line for line rendition would tend to feebleness in some lines and too much forced compression in others, and it concluded by saying, "Mr. Dwight is superior to his associates, and it would have been better to omit the poems of his friends than to destroy the unity of the work by the introduction of different styles". This criticism, however, is not convincing, since practically four-fifths of the work is Dwight's, and in reading the versions of the other translators, one is not conscious of any greater change of style than the variety of the poems themselves demands. Dwight's work is careful, easy, and rhythmic; in the *Parables* and *Epigrams* he has reproduced the vigorous expression and condensation of thought extremely well. Frothingham, in *The Song of the Fates* from *Iphigenia,* has preserved wonderfully the solemn tones and elevation of style of the original. The four selections by Clarke are finely

translated, especially the Orphic Sayings, which retain well the sententious style of Goethe's lines as shown in *Destiny:* According as the sun and planets saw,

From their bright thrones, the moment of thy birth,

Such is thy Destiny: and by that Law

Thou must go on—and on—upon the earth.

Such *must* thou be; Thyself thou canst not fly;

So still do Sibyls speak, have Prophets spoken.

The living stamp, received from Nature's die,

No time can change, no art has ever broken.

or *Hope:*

Yet shall these gates unfold, these walls give way.

These barriers, rooted in the ancient hill,

Are firm as primal rock; but rocks decay;

One essence moves in life and freedom still;

Through cloud, and mist, and storm, to upper day

Lifts the sad heart, weak thoughts, and fainting will;

Through every zone she ranges unconfined;

She waves her wing—we leave time, space behind!

These versions do not disturb the reader by their forced Thymes or their awkward inversions nor make it constantly evident that they have been transplanted from another language. In places they lack the loftiness or sincerity of the original, and often the sound and sense could not be so perfectly adapted to each other as in the German. A few selections will serve to show their value.

To the Moon, by Dwight:

Fillest hill and vale again,

Still with softening light!

Loosest from the world's cold chain

All my soul tonight!

Spreadest round me far and nigh,

Soothingly thy smile;

From thee as from friendship's eye,

Sorrow shrinks the while.

Less successful was his rendering of

The King of Thule:

There was a king in Thule
Till death a constant soul;
His queen, she loved him truly,
And left him a golden bowl.

Nought prized he half so dearly;
He drained it at every bout;
His eyes ran o'er sincerely,
As oft as he drank thereout.

There stood th' old toper,—slowly
Draining life's last, he stood,—
And the cup he kept so holy
He hurled into the flood.

Further on we have Hedge's version of *The Erlking,* which follows the German closely and is one of the best of the many translations of that poem:

Who rideth. so late through the night wind wild?

It Is the father with his child;
He has the little one well in his arm;
He holds him safe, and he folds him warm.

"Come, lovely boy, come go with me;

Such merry plays I will play with thee;

Many a bright flower grows on the strand,

And my mother has many a gay garment at hand."

"I love thee; thy beauty has ravished my sense;
And willing or not, I will carry thee hence!"

"O father, the Erlking now puts forth his arm!
O father, the Erlking has done me harm!"

Since the translators were more interested in Goethe the man than in Goethe the poet, they have done better justice to his unrhymed, dithyrambic measures than to the rhymed lyrics and ballads. Here they have reproduced far more of the original beauty, richness, and melody of the lines than in the other poems, as can be seen in Dwight's translation of *The Song of the Spirits over the Waters:*

The soul of man is
Like the water;
From heaven it cometh,
To heaven it mounteth,
And thence at once

'T must back to earth,
Forever changing
Wind is water's
Amorous wooer;
Wind from its depths
Upheaves the wild waves.
Soul of a mortal,
How like thou to water!
Fate of a mortal,
How like to the wind!

or his version of the *Limits of Humanity:*

When the All-Holy
Father Eternal,
With indifferent hand,
From clouds rolling o'er us,
Sows his benignant
Lightnings around us,
Humbly I kiss the hem of his garment,
Filled with the awe of
A true-hearted child.

Some of the best and truest translating was done in these poems under the caption, *God, Soul, and World,* as may be seen in this final example, *One and All* by Dwight:

How yearns the solitary soul
To melt into the boundless whole,
And find itself again at peace.
The blind desire, the impatient will,
The restless thoughts and plans are still;
We yield ourselves—and wake in bliss.

World-Spirit, come, our spirits firing!
Forevermore to thee aspiring,
We but obey our nature's call.
Good angels feelingly persuade us,
And heaven-taught masters gently lead us
To Him who made and maketh all.

To re-create the old creation,
All things work on in fast rotation,
Lest aught grow fixed, and change resist;
And what was not shall spring to birth,
As purest sun or painted earth.
God's universe may know no rest.
It must go on, creating, changing,
Through endless shapes forever ranging;
And rest we only *seem* to see.
Th' Eternal lives through all revolving;

For all must ever keep dissolving,
Would it continue still to be!

Taken as a whole, this volume shows appreciation, enthusiasm, and conscientious desire to interpret carefully. It sometimes lacks spontaneity and true Goethean grace of style, and it has striking inequalities, but the thought of the poet has not been sacrificed to mere gratification of the ear. From the point of view of workmanship and choice of poems, it is far better than anything that had preceded it and most of the attempts which followed it. It may rightfully be considered a very strong agency in helping to establish a truer knowledge of Goethe's shorter poems in America.

No other attempt was made to bring out a volume of Goethe's poems until 1853, when one was published in London by Edgar A. Bowring. Since it has been the basis of

"An edition of the translated poems of Goethe by E. A. Bowring, in 1846, is mentioned in Goedeke's *Grundrisa,* in E. Oswald's *Bibliography,* and in the British Museum *Catalog,* but I have not been able to substantiate the fact that any of Bowring's translations were published at that time. Bowring himself, in his preface to the edition of 1853, speaks of it as the original edition. The edition of 1846 is sometimes mentioned as a part of the *Bohn Library,* but the *Bohn Library* was not established until 1847. A letter from the firm of G. Bell & Co., London (publishers of the *Bohn Standard Library* since 1864), states that in their opinion no edition of Bowring's translations of Goethe's poems appeared before 1853, when an edition was issued by Parker & Sons, London; this edition, with the addition of *Hermann and Dorothea* and a larger number of the poems of the *Divan,* appeared as Vol. VII of *Bohn's Library* in 1874. See Bibliography *C,* no. 2.

Any facts concerning the life of Edgar A. Bowring have been so difficult to ascertain and so widely scattered that I append here the few that were obtained. His father, Sir John Bowring, is often mentioned in the journals of his day. He was a fine linguist, a great traveller, a prominent man in public life, and translated many of the classics into English. The son Edgar was born in Exeter, England, and spent much of his life abroad with his father; he was educated entirely on the continent and had a thorough knowledge of German. Before translating Goethe's poems in 1853, he had translated two volumes of Alfierl's tragedies, Heine's poems, Schiller's poems and Goethe's minor plays, all of which were incorporated and are still published in *Bohn's Standard Library,* London. Bowring continued to do this sort of work until his death in 1880.

all the volumes of Goethe's poems in English translation edited since 1853, it deserves full discussion. It is far from being absolutely complete, but it contains the translation of nearly four hundred of the shorter poems. The date of composition is stated with each poem, and some brief explanatory notes are added. This volume found a very ready reception, was broadly circulated and widely reviewed, and remains today practically the only volume of Goethe's poems in circulation in English. Every volume of Goethe's shorter poems published in the various editions of Goethe's complete works, as well as the eclectic compilation issued separately, both in England and America, has without exception taken at least two hundred and fifty versions from Bowring and added less than a hundred from other translators. Some of the poems have never been rendered into English by anyone but Bowring, so that the English reading world is to a large extent dependent upon his work. It is then the more to be regretted that as an interpretation of Goethe's thought, style, and delicacy of expression, these versions are so unsatisfactory. The author has tried to render the poems very literally and yet without change of metre; the results are the same for him as for so many of his predecessors; the lines are heavy and mechanical and lacking in grace and melody. Very little of the delicacy and nothing of the brilliance of the originals is left, and there is scarcely a line which seems to be the spontaneous expression of a poetic genius. There lies the great fault in Bowring's work: as a word-for-

word translation of the poems, little fault is to be found with them; as a representation of Goethe's lyric How far from complete even Bowring's collection is can best be shown by a few comparative statements. Over against roughly 2500 of Goethe's "poems" (inclusive of the *Divan)* Bowring has less than 400. To be sure, the great majority of those omitted are the short epigrammatic pieces. As compared with the five volumes of the *JubilSums-Ausgabe,* Bowring, especially in the edition of 1853, goes hardly at all beyond the content of the first two volumes, which alone however contain about 750 numbers. The important groups best represented in Bowring are the *Lieder, Gesellige Lieder, Balladen, Antiker Form sich nUhernd* (Including *Elegieen* and *Venetianische Epigramme), Vermischte Qedichte, Sonette, Parabolisch,* and, less extensively, *Epigrammatisch* and *Lyrisches.* Here few of the most valuable poems are lacking. *Kunat* and *Gott und Welt,* however, are quite inadequately represented. See Bibliography C, footnote 72. power and talent, little good can be said for them. This was so well stated by one of JBowring's contemporaries in a criticism in the London Athenaeum, that I quote from it at length:

In September 1851, Mr. Bowring published a translation of Schiller's poems, which, as the preface stated, was the labour of a few months only, in such leisure moments as could be spared from other occupations of a busy period. He then proceeded to translate Goethe, of whose poems a selection, amounting to some four hundred pieces, has been offered to the public at an interval of less than two years from the appearance of his Schiller. Considering the extreme difficulty—if not the impossibility—of rendering these poems "in the original metres", so as to preserve even a partial likeness of the German author, the time allotted to the task would have seemed unaccountably short, even had the translator devoted it wholly to that one undertaking. This however can not have been the case with Mr. Bowring. Besides his employ-

ment under the Royal Commissioners, he is understood to hold a place in a government office. The period therefore allowed for his translation of Goethe must be reduced considerably within the narrow limit above mentioned; and the result is, that an attempt, the subject of which is the chief poet of his country, and its matter of a kind beyond all others requiring a deliberate exercise of skill, taste and judgment, has been run through in a little more time than it would have taken merely to transcribe the original text.

Of all forms of poetry the lyric yields most reluctantly to the process of translation; of all modern compositions in that form, Goethe's are perhaps the least suited for a hasty trial of this process. This condition arises from two qualities which constitute a part of their rare excellence:—from a pregnancy, namely of substance in which every thought is significant and every word essential; and from a perfection of form in which every line flows with exquisite harmony and the art of composition is only felt In the consummate graces of apparent simplicity and ease. To repeat such masterpieces at the expense of such essential qualities is simply to deface them altogether.

Such being the description, it will surprise no one, least of all will it surprise those who have read these poems in Goethe's own pages, to learn that the result of Mr. Bowrings ready reckoning with the poet is far from satisfactory. He has obviously a facile pen, with much address in rhyming, and is not without a feeling of certain beauties of his original; and it may be believed that *"London Athenaeum,* 1853, no. 1358, p. 1319.

with due exertion of his best powers and a thorough study of his author, he might have approached more nearly than he has done to a becoming treatment of Goethe's poems. As it is, the version he produces is entirely insufficient, and particularly because his English fails the most in respect of those very features which have been described above as essential merits of the German. He is lax where Goethe is succinct; vague where he is precise; and substitutes for his exquisite melody, clear sense, and graceful ease.of numbers, strains which are unmusical, obscure diction, and lines disfigured with Inversions. Of these faults, a part may be owing to the design of retaining the original meters, but as these.devices also occur in pieces to which this disadvantage does not apjply, the defect in such cases must arise from the want either of a itaste alive to the felicitous propriety of Goethe's diction or of that just respect for the author which would have enforced the duty of taking pains to follow him. In many instances, too, from Goethe's.verbal meaning, another entirely different, and of course less suitable, has been introduced; and this license occurs oftenest in pieces where the lyrical structure is the most delicate and difficult—with a most unfortunate effect.

It has already been said that the task of translating Goethe is arduous in the extreme. Had it been imposed on the translator by some necessity, there would have been reason to make large allowance for the failure. But in this instance there can have been no constraint to account for so ambitious an attempt, still less any necessity for hastening to publish its results without allowing time for revision and retouching, to say nothing of the particular respect due to the consummate works of a genius of the highest order. It would have given Mr. Bowring an idea of the nature of his enterprise and a view of the relative proportion between himself and the European poets of the highest rank which would have dissuaded him from hurried translations and from giving them in a crude state to the public, in this instance, and in the previous case of Schiller.

The quality of Bowring's translations seems to justify in large part the sharpness of this criticism. So far as could be ascertained, none of these translations had ever appeared in any magazines previous to their publication in book form, and so were not subjected to criticism or revision. In the preface to the second edition, in 1874, Bowring stated that he had made "whatever im

provements suggested themselves in the original version", but a comparison of the two editions reveals no marked improvements, while in some cases the earlier versions were the better.

Bowring's translations are not like a veil which lets us see faintly the finer lines of the figure underneath, but they are rather like a mask which hides or distorts the original lines. The life, the feeling, the inspiration are not even dimly reproduced. In Shelley's version of *The Mayday Night* there are lines which, though not exactly like the original, so thoroughly ring with its spirit that they are almost a re-creation of Goethe's thought:

Und die langen Felsennasen.
Wie sie schnarchen, wie sie blasen
And the rugged crags, ho, ho,
How they snort, and how they Wow

But flights of this kind are not to be found in Bowring's collection. His best work is done in the parables, epigrams, elegies, and sententious stanzas, yet even here we feel a lack of earnestness. The following may serve as examples of the best of these: *Poetry:*

God to his untaught children sent
Law, order, knowledge, art from high,
And every heavenly favour lent,
The world's hard lot to qualify.
They knew not how they should behave,
For all from Heav'n stark-naked came;
But Poetry their garments gave,
And then not one had cause for shame.
Human Feelings:
Ah, ye gods! ye great immortals,
In the spacious heavens above us!
Would ye on this earth hut give us
Steadfast minds and dauntless courage
We, oh kindly ones, would leave you
All your spacious heavens above us!
For Ever:
The happiness that man, whilst prison'd here,
Is wont with heavenly rapture to compare,—
The harmony of Truth, from wavering clear,—
Of Friendship that is free from doubting care,—
The light which in stray thoughts alone can cheer
The wise,—the bard alone in visions

fair,—
In my best hours I found in *her* all this,
And made mine own, to my exceeding bliss.
or the eighth of the *Venetian Epigrams:*
I would liken this Gondola unto a soft-rocking cradle,
And the chest on its deck seems a vast coffin to be.
Yes, 'tween the cradle and coffin, we totter and waver forever
On the mighty canal, careless our lifetime is spent.

Most truly of all are the *Roman Elegies* rendered:
Speak, ye stones, I entreat! Oh speak, ye palaces lofty!
Utter a word, oh ye streets! Wilt thou not Genius awake?
All that thy sacred walls, eternal Rome, hold within them
Teemeth with life; but to *me,* all is still, silent, and dead.

When we consider the lyrics proper, we find only a few that are poetical, as for instance *The Bliss of Sorrow:*
Never dry, never dry,
Tears that eternal love sheddeth!
How dreary, how dead, doth the world still appear,
When only half-dried on the eye is the tear.
Never dry, never dry,
Tears that unhappy love sheddeth!
Here the lines are smooth and flowing but the idea of the original is not quite correctly conveyed, and some of the expressions are hum-drum rather than pathetic. The best translation of the collection is the *Night Song*:
When on thy pillow lying,
Half listen, I implore,
And at my lute's soft sighing,
Sleep on! what wouldst thou more?
For at my lute's soft sighing
The stars their blessings pour
On feelings never-dying;
Sleep on! what wouldst thou more?
Aside from these that have just been mentioned, there are few which show that Bowring appreciated the subtler difficulties to be overcome. Let us take the *Heathrose,* and we find that it has been quite crushed in its transit from one language to the other:

Once a boy a Rosebud spied,
Heathrose fair and tender,
All array'd In youthful pride,—
Quickly to the spot he hied,
Ravished by her splendor.
Rosebud, roesbud, rosebud red,
Heathrose fair and tender!

Said the boy, "I'll now pick thee,
Heathrose, fair and tender!"
Said the rosebud, "I'll prick thee,
So that thou'lt remember me,
Ne'er will I surrender!"
Rosebud—etc.

Now the cruel boy must pick
Heathrose fair and tender;
Rosebud did her best to prick,—
Vain 'twas 'gainst her fate to kick—
She must needs surrender.
Rosebud—etc.

Scarcely a suspicion of the beautiful ballad strain of the original can be detected in this dry and spiritless rendering of the *Erlking:*

Who rides there so late through the night dark and drear?
The father it is, with his infant so dear;
He holdeth the boy tightly clasped in his arm,
He holdeth him safely, he keepeth him warm.
"I love thee, I'm charmed by thy beauty, dear boy!
And if thou'rt unwilling, then force I'll employ."
"My father, my father, he seizes me fast,
Full sorely the Erlking has hurt me at last."
The father now gallops with terror half wild,
He grasps in his arms the poor shuddering child;
He reaches his courtyard with toil and with dread,—
The child in his arms finds he motionless, dead.

Let us compare with Mangan's singing measures (which were quoted earlier) Bowring's prosy version of the *DeathLament of the Noble Wife of Asan Aga,* and it will be quite tc the detriment of the later translator:

What is yonder white thing in the forest?
Is it snow, or can it swans perchance be?

Were it snow, e'er this it had been melted,
Were it swans, they all away had hasten'd.
Snow, in truth, It is not, swans it is not,
'Tis the shining tents of Asan Aga.
He within is lying sorely wounded;
To him come his mother and his sister;
Bashfully his wife delays to come there.

As for the "Oden in freien Rhythmen", nothing of the noble freedom and spontaneity is left, they seem to be merely chopped-up prose, as may be seen from the following specimens: *The Boundaries of Humanity:*

When the primeval
All-holy Father
Sows with tranquil hand
From clouds as they roll,
Bliss-spreading lightnings
Over the earth,
Then do I kiss the last
Hem of his garment
While by a childlike awe
Filled is my breast.

or *My Goddess:*

Say, which Immortal
Merits the highest reward?
With none contend I,
But I will give it
To the aye-changing,
Ever-moving
Wondrous daughter of Jove,
His best-beloved offspring,
Sweet Phantasy.

After having read and studied Bowring's volume carefully, our feeling on leaving it is one of distress at its inadequacy. It offers little tangible ground for criticism, and yet it is not in any way a representation of Goethe's work. It not only does not suggest or reflect Goethe's lyrical genius, but it turns away, repelled, those who are eager to know that side of Goethe's greatness. The Goethean influence is strong in the life of German students, and they can and do turn to Goethe for counsel and guidance on the great intellectual problems of his day. German writings are constantly enriched by quotations from Goethe's poems, but among all of Bowring's versions there is scarcely one of sufficient loftiness to serve as a quotation in a serious theme. His verse

is rarely stirring, and although generally speaking it is singularly close to the original, it is too frequently formal and artificial, preserving but little of the gracefulness by which the German is distinguished.

Much more successful, although much more incomplete, was the volume of translations by W. E. Aytoun and Sir Theodore Martin, *Poems and Ballads of Goethe,TM* which appeared in 1859 in London, Edinburgh, and New York. Bowring's

"William Edmonstoune Aytoun, (1813-1865), was born in Edinburgh. His parents were people of literary tastes, and he began to write verses at an early age. While studying in Germany he began to make translations from the German for the English magazines. From 1840 to 1844 he worked in collaboration with Theodore Martin and produced *Bon Gaultier's Ballads* (13th edition issued in 1887). In 184445 they translated anonymously *The Ballads and Minor Poems of Goethe* for *Blackwood's Magazine* (V: 56—57), on whose staff Aytoun was then serving. In 1845 he was made Professor of Rhetoric and Belles-lettres in the University of Edinburgh. He continued his translations, and in 1859 this volume was Anally published.

"Sir Theodore Martin, (1816-1909), was born and lived all his life in Edinburgh. He contributed poetry to *Fraser's* and *Taifs Magazines* at an early age under the name of "Bon Gaultier". From 1840 to 1859, he collaborated with Aytoun in various literary ventures. Most of his life was spent in making translations, publishing and revising them: 1838, Rabelais' *Gargantua and Pantagruel;* 1844, Goethe's *Ballads and Poems;* 1854, Oehlenschlager's *Corregio;* 1859, Goethe's *Ballads and Poems;* 1863, Dante's *Vita Nuova;* 1865, *Faust,* part I; 1866, *Faust,* part II; 1878, Heine's *Poems;* 1889, *The Song of the Belt* and other translations from Schiller, Goethe, Wieland. Uhland, and others; 1893, Goethe's *Roman Elegies* complete (published by the English Goethe Society, VII:71-84.) See Bibliography *C,* no. 3.

collection gave nearly four hundred poems; this volume offers but one hundred and eight, selected as follows: songs and lyrics, forty; ballads, twenty; "In the manner of the Antique", twenty-three; miscellaneous poems, twenty-five. Both Aytoun and Martin had genuine poetic talent and had written original lyrics and ballads, both attempted these translations from love of the task, and both worked slowly and sympathetically. A large number of their versions had previously appeared in various magazines and had been criticised and thoroughly revised before they were printed in book form. When the book appeared, it was at once favorably reviewed and widely circulated, a second edition was published in 1860, and a third and revised edition in 1907 and 1908. These later editions were likewise favorably reviewed by the various critics.

In and of themselves these versions are readable and pleasing, showing taste and poetic feeling. The original feeling has been excellently reproduced in the ballads, which retain to a large extent the original metre, the feminine rhymes, and the poetic flow of phrase, as can be seen in the following examples: *The Dance of the Dead:*

The warder looked down at dead of night,
On the graves where the dead were sleeping,
And, clearly as day, was the pale moonlight
O'er the quiet churchyard creeping.
One after another the gravestones began
To heave and to open, and woman and man
Rose up in their ghastly apparel!

as *The God and the Bayadere:*
Mahadeh, earth's lord, descending,
To its mansions comes again,
That like man with mortal blending,
He may feel their joy and pain.
Stoops to try life's varied changes
And with human eyes to see,
Ere he praises or avenges,
What their fitful lot may be.

He has passed through the city, has looked on them all;
He has watched o'er the great, nor forgotten the small,

And at evening went forth on his journey so free.

The Doleful Lay of the Wife of Asan Aga is better than Bowring's but not as true as Mangan's (see pp. 44 and 63).

What is yon so white beside the greenwood?
Is it snow or flight of cygnets resting?
Were it snow, ere now it had been melted:
Were It swans, ere now the flock had left us.
Neither snow nor swans are resting yonder,
'Tis the glittering tent of Asan Aga,
Faint he lies from wounds in stormy battle.
There his mother and his sisters seek him
But his wife hangs back for shame and comes not.

In some cases the directness and simplicity of the original have been too much elaborated, but even here there is a pleasing rhythm, and the reader does not have that sense of artificiality which has been found in so many of the previous translations. Let us select a few of the most striking examples of this elaboration; we shall find that the general effect of the poem is not spoiled by it because the rhythm of the lines and the sense of the words are natural.

The third stanza of *The Fisher:*
The sun and ladye-moon they lave
Their tresses in the main,
And breathing freshness from the wave
Come doubly bright again.
The deep blue sky so moist and clear
Hath it for thee no lure,
Does thine own face not woe thee down
Unto our waters pure.

or *The Limits of" Humanity:*
When the Creator,
The Great, the Eternal,
Sows with indifferent
Hand from the rolling
Clouds, o'er the earth
His lightnings in blessing,
I kiss the nethermost
Hem of his garment
Lowly inclining
In infantine awe.

or the first *Wanderer's Night Song:* TM
Child of Heaven, who soothing calm
On every pain and sorrow pourest,
And a doubly healing balm
Find'st for him whose need is sorest,
Oh, I am of life aweary!
What availeth its unrest—
Pain that flndeth no release,
Joy that at the best is dreary?
Gentle Peace,
Come, o come into my breast!

Although this version is faulty, yet it is truer than Bowring's translation:
Thou who comest from on high,
Who all woes and sorrows stillest,
Who for two-fold misery,
Hearts with two-fold balsam fillest,
Would this constant strife would cease!
What are pain and rapture now?
Blissful Peace,
To my bosom hasten thou.

Not so many versions of the second *Wanderer's Night Song (Ueber alien Gipfeln)* were found as of the first, but of them all Martin succeeds in bringing out most clearly the full idea of the original lines, which are so simple and so elusive that they almost defy transposition into another tongue:

Peace breathes along the shade Of every hill.
The tree tops of the glade
Are hushed and still.

Of all the versions of this poem (see Bibliography *E*, no. 72) Longfellow's has been generally accepted as the best and is usually given In the eclectic volumes:
"Thou that from the heavens art,
Every pain and sorrow stillest,
And the doubly wretched heart
Doubly with refreshment fillest,
I am weary with contending.
Why this rapture and unrest?
Peace, descending,' , Come, ah, come into my breast!"

All woodland murmurs cease.
The birds to rest within the brake are gone,
Be patient, weary heart, anon
Thou, too, shalt be at peace.

Longfellow made a very close translation, but it seems to lack something of the dignity of Goethe's lines:
Over all the hilltops

Is quiet now,
In all the treetops
Hearest thou
Hardly a breath.
The birds are asleep In the trees,
Wait, soon like these,
Thou, too, shalt rest.

Later Bowring translated it, but in his version the whole idea of the poem seems contracted and lacks lightness:
Hushed on the hill
Is the breeze,
Scarcely by the zephyr
The trees
Softly are pressed:
The woodbird's asleep on the bough.
Wait, then, and thou
Soon wilt find rest.

In all the translations which they made, Aytoun and Martin succeeded least in those "After the manner of the Antique". *Die Geschwister* is the best and truest; in the others they reproduced neither the spirit nor the rhythm. One reviewer exclaimed, "The series entitled 'Antiker Form sich nahernd' should be designated 'Antiker Form sich entfernend' ".

As seems inevitable in translation, the feeling is not so spontaneous and the emotions are less stirring, but taken as a whole these versions have life and the ring of inspiration. Sometimes the reader forgets that they are translations, and rarely does he have the impression that words and phrases have been used merely for the sake of rhyme. Some of these *"London Athenaeum,* 1859, p. 216.
versions seem to have found the original spirit quite completely, as for instance *The Song of the Spirits over the Waters:*
The soul of man
It is like water,
From heaven it cometh,
To heaven it mounteth,
And again
Still interchanging
Evermore returns to earth.
Aloft it shoots,
A star in brightness,
From the beetling
Wall of rock,
Then in waves
Of graceful vapour

On the glistening
Basalt, dustlike,
Falls, and touched and
Touching lightly,
Like a veil
It showers down softly,
Whispering to its craggy base.
or the *May Song:*
How gloriously gleameth
All nature to me!
How bright the sun beameth!
How laughs out the lea!
Rich blossoms are bursting
The branches among,
And all the gay greenwood
Is ringing with song!
There is radiance and rapture
That naught can destroy,
Oh earth, in thy sunshine,
Oh heart, in thy joy!

Taken as a whole these translations are the best that we have in English; their easy flow bears scarcely a trace of the labor or constraint of translation, while the true spirit of the original is well maintained, whether in pathos or humor. They form really a valuable contribution towards a truer understanding of Goethe's lyrics.

The last collection of Goethe's poems in translation which appeared before 1860 was that by "William Grassatt Thomas, entitled *"The Minor Poetry of Goethe,* selections from his songs, ballads, and other lesser poems.' ' The introduction to the volume and the explanatory notes show much study of the subject and great appreciation of Goethe's work. The choice of poems is peculiar, and one finds included here a number not attempted by any one else and not usually found in the general collections of Goethe's verse, as for instance the early poems written in Leipzig, those relating to Frederica, to Lotte, to Lili, and to Frau von Stein; some of these last were taken from Goethe's letters, not having been included by Goethe himself in his collected poems. Thomas also translated nearly all of the lyrics from *Wilhelm Meister,* four from *Faust,* eight sonnets, three elegies, eleven ballads, seven parables, twentjfive epigrams, and quite a number of miscellaneous poems, making about

one hundred and thirty poems in the collection. He does not indicate anywhere that he desired to complement any of the existing collections, but seems merely to have followed the line of his fancy, in making his selection. In tne introduction he says: "The poems in this collection belong for the most part to Goethe's earlier years, his later lyrical writings being deficient in the warmth and simplicity which distinguish the productions of his youth". If these versions reproduced anything of the warmth and simplicity of the originals, they would form a very decided addition to the completer comprehension of the minor poems. A few quotations from the volume will show, however, the lack of poetry and the general weakness of these versions: From *The Wild Rose:*
Once a youth a rosebud found,
Rosebud on the lea!
So with morning beauty crowned,
Nearer he did quickly bound,
See Bibliography *C,* no. 4.
Saw't delighted he.
Rosebud, rosebud, rosebud red,
Rosebud on the lea!
from *The Minstrel:*
"Without the gate what hear I there,
What on the drawbridge sound?
The music let before us here
Within our hall resound."
Thus spoke the king, the page he sped,
The youth returned, the monarch said,
"Bring here the old man in!"
from *The Two Threats:*
My maiden I did after go,
Once deep within the wood,
And fell upon her neck, when Oh!
She threatened scream she would.
and lastly from *The King of Thule:*
In Thule there lived of old
A king true to the grave,
To whom a cup of gold
His mistress dying gave.
He cherished nothing more,
He drained it every draught,
With tears his eyes ran o'er
Whenever he from it quaffed.

I have not been able to find any reviews or criticisms of this book in the magazines at the time it appeared, which would not argue well for its quality. A rather close and thorough study of it has shown that while most of the translations are close to the meaning of the original, there is scarcely one that could be selected for the excellence of its poetic form or tone. The general style is restrained and uninspired, numerous inversions cause unnatural English constructions, and as a consequence there are few flowing lines. It bears no closer resemblance to the original lyrics than a dried botanical specimen does to the flower growing in the field. No translations from Thomas's book have been found in any of the eclectic volumes or later anthologies.

There is one other volume of Goethe's poems which has had a widespread circulation, at least in America. Throughout these pages it has been referred to as "the eclectic volume' ', and since most of the versions included in this volume, in fact all but nine of the poems, were translated before 1860, it may properly be considered here. If a Goethe student finds the Bowring volume as published in the *Bdhn Standard Library* insufficient for his needs, the only alternative, if he wishes to quote in English from Goethe's lyrics, is this eclectic volume, because Mangan's, Dwight's, and Aytoun-Martin's are, I believe, out of print. It does not really offer us a great amount of new material, since of the entire number, 274 poems are from Bowring, 68 from Aytoun-Martin, 5 by Professor Leopold Noa, 3 by Edward Chawner, 2 by Dwight, 2 by George H. Lewes, and 1 each by Longfellow, Carlyle, Morrison, Dale, Sprague, and Bayard Taylor. Exactly who made this selection is not quite certain, but it is probable that it was made by F. H. Hedge and Professor Noa, since it first appeared in their set of ten volumes of Goethe's works in English, in 1882. The selection was probably made from all of the various translations then at hand, and while it is not the best selection that could be made, it is an improvement over Bowring's volume.

With the many translations of individual poems which this investigation and other recent studies have brought to light, a far better eclectic volume could

now be compiled. Of course it is a much mooted question whether or not an eclectic edition is better than one which is all the work of one translator. What has been done thus far seems to show that no one translator can adequately master all the forms and styles which Goethe penned. It would seem that since Goethe was so many-sided in his genius and wrote throughout so many years, in so many different moods, that many translators would be more apt to catch the varied spirit and chang See Bibliography C, footnote 72 for contents and authors. See Bibliography B, no. 2. ing atmosphere of these different lyrics than any single person could. However that may be, it is to be hoped that some improved edition may soon be forthcoming for English readers. It is Interesting to note here the translations used in the first volume of the *German Classics,* published in 1913 in twenty volumes. Volume I is devoted to Goethe's poems. Of the twenty-six shorter poems given, seventeen are by Bowring—and by no means his best ones,— three by Aytoun-Martin, six by recent translators, A. I. Coleman and C. W. Stork. Thus even this last and finest effort "to correct the narrow and inadequate view which the English speaking world has of German literature", as the editors say, is based mainly on the work done prior to 1860. The editors go on to say that "the crux of the whole undertaking lies in the correctness and adequacy of the translations". Certainly Bowring"s translations cannot be considered the best that we have from either of these points of view. *The German Classics* of the nineteenth and twentieth centuries. Masterpieces of German Literature translated into English. Editor-inchief, Kuno Francke; Ass't Editor, W. G. Howard. XX vols. German IPub. Society, New York City, 1913. Vols. I, II, *Goethe.* COMPLETE SETS OF GOETHE'S WOEKS
A few words might fittingly be said here about the translations used in the complete sets of Goethe's works, as circulated in this country and in England. The investigation concerning the volume of poems in each of these sets led

to an examination of the other volumes and brought out some interesting facts. A detailed statement has been made in connection with Bibliography B, p. 84. It was found that here, as with the volume of poems, most of the work of translating was done before 1860. Very little new material has been added since then, and very little revision has been made since the first editions published by the *Bohn Standard Library.* The Bohn edition is the only one current in England; it began with one volume of Goethe's *Dramatic Works* in 1847, and has continued to publish and add to Goethe's work. In 1908 a Bohn edition of 14 volumes was published; in this the recent additions are mostly of the prose works and letters, while the poems and dramas remain as in the early editions. In America various editions *de luxe,* elaborate, simple, and cheap, have been offered, beginning with the reprints of the early Bohn edition and continuing to a 14 volume edition in 1912. Many of these would lead the reader, librarian, or purchaser to believe that he was obtaining something new in scholarship and research, or at least in translation, but a comparison of the various editions shows that very few of them offer anything new or revised. In most cases the American editions are entirely identical with the early, unrevised Bohn translations, to which no acknowledgment has been made. In a,number of instances there is no way of knowing who the translators are, since no names are mentioned on title-page or in the body of volumes, so that only a word-for-word comparison with other versions will establish the translator. In several editions the title See Bibliography B, no. 1, for contents of 14 vols. See Bibliography B, no. 7, b.
page would lead the reader to understand that the whole set was the work of such famous writers as Longfellow, Carlyle, Scott, and Bayard Taylor. As a matter of fact, in all of the nine or ten volumes of these sets, Scott translated the *Gotz,* Carlyle the *Wilhelm Meister,* Longfellow the two *Wanderer's Night Songs,* and Bayard Taylor *The King of Thule,* otherwise the sets are quite iden-

tical with the Bohn translations. Another edition of 14 volumes, which has had a considerable circulation, advertises to be the work of Samuel Taylor Coleridge, John Storer Cobb, Anna Swanwick, *and others.* An examination of the contents fails to show any translation by Coleridge; *Beineke Fox* is by Cobb, and *Egmont* by Swanwick (1850), leaving virtually thirteen volumes to the "others", all anonymous translators, who turn out to be our old friends the early Bohn translators.

Surely since 1860, with the material made accessible in recent years and with the more thorough study which has been given Goethe's writings, here is a branch of work worthy the attention of Goethe students: To see that a new edition, entirely revised, made up from the best translations and based on the soundest scholarship of recent years, with the translators frankly mentioned and all authorities stated, be put into circulation. The translator's art and the editor's responsibility have been regarded too lightly. Since the study of international literary influences has made such a growth, the value of translations is more truly recognized as being of immense use to students of comparative literature. These translations must be an exact, faithful, and spirited representative of the original writer. There is now more than ever a demand for a truthful, accurate, and scholarly edition of Goethe's complete works, including his shorter poems.

See Bibliography *B,* no. 2 and 3.

See Bibliography *B,* no. 7, a, b. c.

SUMMARY OF THE PERIOD PRIOR TO 1860

Looking over the whole field with regard to Goethe's shorter poems in England and America, the results seem decidedly negative. In spite of the large amount of material that has come to hand, we might say that prior to 1860—and even up to the present—Goethe as a supreme lyric poet is not known and cannot be so known, if it depends upon the translation of his poems.

In the early years of the nineteenth century, when the interest of English readers lay in the direction of ballad po-

etry, a number of his ballads were variously translated and widely read: *The Erlking, The Fisher, The King of Thule, Mignon, The Heather Rose, The Violet, The Harper, The Apprentice in Magic,* and the *Song of the Imprisoned Count.* These were perhaps the best translations made at any time. Then came a very few of the early lyrics, but further than these the interest did not go. Somewhat later, when Goethe was recognized as the leader of a new literary movement, a few of his poems, such as *Prometheus, Mahomet's Song, The Song of the Spirits over the Waters, My Goddess, The Divine,* and *The Limits of Humanity,* received attention in certain literary circles of both countries, but never became popularly known. And for that matter, what lyrics of Goethe ever have become popularly known in English translation, except possibly the first five ballads named? Aside from the poems mentioned above, only ten poems appeared ten times or more in the combined English and American literature for the sixty years under consideration. This certainly cannot be called general popularity or even general recognition.

Fortunately, the lyrics included in *Faust* have had a much *"Nearness of the Beloved,* 26; *New Love, New Life,* 11; *To Belinda,* 11; *Comfort in Tears,* 10; *Spirifs Greeting,* 15; *To a Golden Heart,* 11; *Wanderer's Night Song,* 12; *To the Moon,* 16; *Vanitas,* 14; *The Wanderer,* 11.

broader and more constant circulation, and have been more carefully worked over. But even these are connected with Goethe's name as the author of *Faust* and not as a lyric poet. The same distinction might be made with regard to the poems in *Wilhelm Meister.* Now and again some devoted student had tried to impress upon English readers the greatness of Goethe as a lyric poet and had had some success. This idea was greatly strengthened toward the end of our period, in 1855, when George Henry Lewes's *Life of Goethe* was published, which emphasized Goethe's lyric gift. This biography was one of the most widely read and reviewed books of the time. In it Lewes said:

The Faust and the lyrics suffice to give Goethe preeminence among the poets of modern times, Shakespeare excepted; and had they stood alone as representatives of his genius, no one would ever have disputed his rank. The lyrics are the best known of his work and have by their witchery gained the admiration of even his antagonists. One hears very strange opinions about him and his works but one never hears anything except praise of the minor poems. They are instinct with life and beauty against which no prejudice can stand. But one and all are inaccessible through translation; therefore I cannot attempt to give the English reader an idea of them; the German reader already has anticipated me, by studying them in the original.

What Lewes, said in 1855 must still stand as true. In Germany all authorities agree that Goethe stands as the first and greatest master in the domain of lyric verse. In England and America this is just as fully recognized. Professor J. G. Robertson, of the University of London, has reiterated this opinion for the English literary world, when he soys:

In what form of poetry did Goethe most excel? Where is he to be found at his best and highest? Most critics will no doubt answer, in the lyric. To say that Goethe was supreme as a lyric poet is only another way of saying that the peculiar strength of the German artistic genius lies in its power to give expression to See Bibliography *D,* no. 71.

"Robertson, J. G., *Goethe and the Twentieth Century,* Cambridge Univ. Press, 1912.

the subjective, and Goethe's genius seems to sum up the qualities which we have learned to associate with the German lyric.—There is a bigness and a universality about his lyric genius before which that of the other poets seems small and personal.

And now how is the English reader to know the beauties, and this bigness, and this universality of these lyrics?

The Goethe lyrics in magazines, in anthologies, and in single volumes appeared with greatest frequency from 1840 to 1855. Most of these translations are now widely scattered and quite inaccessible for the general reader, and most of them seem sadly inadequate in representing Goethe to the foreign reader. The spirit in which the translations were made, especially after Carlyle's work in England, and the writings of the trancendentalists and Unitarians in America, was generally a serious one, which wished to understand the essence of the Goethean thought. To that extent most of the work is commendable, even though the re-shaping of the material into English lyric form was not successful. As has been said, the books of Aytoun-Martin and Mangan are now out of print and give, at the best, only a small portion of these poems in a way that would suggest the charm of the originals and win readers for Goethe either in English or in German, while Bowring and Thomas give versions that are stiff, unpoetical, and lifeless. Thus, even though fifty years have passed, years in which the study and understanding of Goethe have made enormous strides, we have to reiterate Lewes' statement of 1855, and say that in this, his supreme field, Goethe is inaccessible to the English reader. Since Goethe's greatest title to fame rests upon his lyric poems, it seems a serious loss that this important phase of his work must be so meagerly and inadequately known. As the author of *Faust* and of other dramas, as the author of novels, tales, autobiography, and letters, we are able to draw very near to Goethe, in English translations. Any one of the standard sets of Goethe's complete works will convey to us a fairly accurate knowledge of his genius, in all fields *except tJie lyric;* here he is still *terra incognita,*—or worse.

And yet we would not leave the subject feeling that it is all in the shadow. It is encouraging to note how many lovers of literature have tried in some way to make known some part of these lyric beauties. It would probably be hard to find any other foreign author, the translation of whose lyrics has been attempted by so many thoughtful, earnest, and well-known students of literature: John Anster, Mrs. Sarah Austin, George Bancroft, John Blackie, William Cullen Bryant, Thomas Carlyle, W. E. Chan-

ning, J. F. Clarke, Arthur Hugh Clough, Samuel T. Coleridge, John S. Dwight, Margaret Fuller, Fitz-Greene Halleck, Mrs. Felicia Hemans, George Henry Lewes, H. W. Longfellow, Walter Scott, Percy Bysshe Shelley, Harriet Beecher Stowe, Bayard Taylor, John Gr. Whittier. Evidently these minds sensed the fact that here lies hidden valuable material. Certainly such a list indicates that here is a great field for some future worker, and it should act as an inspiration to some qualified person Avith a willingness to subordinate his own gift, who may some day make accessible to the English reader the finest expression of Goethe's genius.

BIBLIOGRAPHIES

A.—Bibliography Of Bibliographies

Adams, O. F. *Brief Handbook of English Authors.* Boston,
Houghton, Mifflin & Co. 1885.
Brief Handbook of American Authors. Bost.,
Houghton, Mifflin & Co. 1885.

Allibones, S. A. *Dictionary of Authors from the Middle Ages to 1859.* 3 vols. Supplement, 2 vols. Edited by J. F. Kirk. London, Triibner, 1859; Philadelphia, Childs, 1891.

American Catalog of Books to 1876. N. Y., Armstrong, 1881. 4.

Anderson, John P. (Of the British Museum.) *Appendix to J. Sime's Life of Goethe* Lond., Scott, 1888. 44 pp. 8.

Anthony Memorial. *A Catalog of the Harris Collection of American Poetry.* Providence, R. I. 1886. 4. Breul, K. H. *A Handy Bibliographical Guide to the Study of German Language and Literature.* Lond.,
Hachette and Co., 1895. 144 pp. 8.
British Catalog of Printed Books. (Goethe vol. in 1888)
Lond., Clowes & Son. 4. *Bulletin of the Public Library* of the City of Boston. XIV: 1. Apr. 1895. (pp. 19-32, Works of and by Goethe). Cairns, W. B. *The Developement of American Literature 1815-1833.* (Bulletin of University of Wisconsin).
Madison. 1898. 87 pp. *Card Catalog* of the Library of Congress. Washington, D. C. *Catalog of German Publications.* Selected and systematically

arranged for W. H. Roller and Jul. Cahlmann.

Lond., 1829. 179 pp. *Classified Catalog* of the Library of the Goethe Society of

Manchester, Eng. Warrington, Mackie & Co. 1894.
pp. 183-209.

Davis, E. Z. *Translation of German Poetry in American Magazines.* Americana-Germanica Press, Phila. 1905. 229 pp.

Edmands, John (Of the Phila. Mercantile Library).
Appendix to Life and Genius of Goethe. Edited by
F. B. Sanborn. Bost., Ticknor. 1886. 33 pp.

Encyclopedia Britannica. Article on *Goethe,* with bibliography, by J. G. Eobertson, 11th edition, 12: 187. 1910-1911.
Article on *Goethe,* with bibliography, by Oscar
Browning, 9th edition, 10: 737. 1879.
English Catalog of Books, 1835-1863. Compiled by S. Low.
Lond., Low. 1864. 910 pp. Fletcher, W. I. *Index to General Literature* (Amer.
Library Ass'n.) 2nd edition, *Goethe,* p. 237. Bost.,
Houghton, Mifflin & Co. 1901. Ooedeke, Karl. *Grundriss zur Geschichte der deutschen Dichtung.* 2. Auflage, Band IV, 419-756. 1891; 3.
Auflage, Band IV, 2. Abteilung, 1. Heft, 1910; 3.
Abteilung, 1. Heft, S. 52-55. 1911. Dresden, Ehler mann.

Goodnight, S. H. *German Literature in American Magazines prior to 1846.* (Bulletin of the University of Wisconsin). Madison, Wis. 1907. 264 pp.

Growell, A. *Three Centuries of English Booh Trade.* Bibliography. N. Y., Greenhalg, 1903.
Handbook for Readers in the Boston Public Library. 9th edition, Bost., 1890. Ill pp.

Haney, J. L. *German Literature in England before 1790.*
Phil., Americana-Germanica Series, Vol. IV, no. 2. 1902. pp. 80-155.

Haertel, M. H. *German Literature in*

American Magazines 1846-1880. (Bulletin of the Univ. of Wisconsin). Madison, Wis. 1908. 188 pp.

Heinemann, W. *A Bibliographical List of the English Translations and Annotated Editions of Goethe's Faust.* Lond., 2nd edition, 1888. 31 pp.

Hirzel, S. *"Verzeichnis einer Goethe-Bibliothek.* Supplemented by von Loeper and von Biedermann. Leip., Hirzel, 1884. 216 pp.

Hoyer, K. *Zur Einfiihrung in die Goethe-Lit.* Gelsen kirchen, 1904. 71 pp. *Index* to Catolog of the Public Library. Bost., Rand &

Avery, 1861.

Kelly, J. *American Catalog of Books, 1861-1871.* 2 vols. N. Y. 1871.

Lancizolle, L. von. *Uebersicht der wichtigsten Schriften von und iiber Goethe.* Tabellarisch geordnet. IV. Teil, Register über G's Werke. Berlin, 1857. 55 pp. 8.

Lieder, F. W. C. *Goethe in England and America.* Additions to E. Oswald's Bibliography. *Journal of Eng. and Ger. Philology,* Urbana, Ill., 1911. X: 535-557.

Matson, H. *References for Literary Workers.* (Goethe, pp. 298-302). Chicago, McClurg, 1893. 8.

Meyer, Friedrich. *Verzeichnis einer Goethe-Bibliothek.* Leip. 1908. 707 pp.

Meyer, R. M. *Grundriss der neuem deutschen Literaturgeschichte.* Berlin, 1902; 2. Auflage, 1907. 312 pp. 8.

Nollen, J. S. *Chronology and Practical Bibliography of Modem German Literature.* Chi. Scott, Foresman & Co. 1903. 118 pp.

Oswald, Eugene. *Goethe in England and America.* Bibliography. 1st edition. English Goethe Society Publications, no. 8. Lond., Nutt, 1899. 2nd edition, revised and enlarged by L. and E. Oswald, English Goethe Society, no. 11. Lond., Moring. 1909. 75 pp.

Oswald, F. W. *German Literature in English Magazines. 1810-1835.* Dissertation, University of "Wisconsin, not yet published, used in ms.

Poole. *Index to Periodical Lit.* Bost., 3rd edition, 18481882.

Rea, T. *Schiller's Drtßmas and Poems in England.* Bibliography. Lond.

, Unwin, 1906. 155 pp.

Roloff, W. E. *German Literature in English Magazines. 1779-1810.* Dissertation, University of Wisconsin, not yet published, used in ms.

Roorbach, 0. A, *Catalog of American Publications,* 1820-1861. N. Y. 4 vols. 1861.

Ruff, P. G. *German Literature in English Magazines, 1835-1860.* Dissertation, University of Wisconsin, not yet published, used in ms.

Thimm, Franz. *Goethe in the British Museum.* Article in *Library Chronicle,* vol. IV, no. 43. 1887.

Tombo, R. Jr. *Englisch-amerikanische Bibliographic* Goethe-Jahrbuch, Bde. 26, 27, 29, 32, 1905-1911. Frankfurt am Main, Riitten u. Loening.

Triibner, N. *Bibliographical Guide to American Literature.* Lond., 1859.

"White, H. S. *Englisch-amerikanische Bibliographic.* Goethe-Jahrbuch, Bde. 8, 9, 10, 11, 12, 1887-1891. Frankfurt am Main. Riitten u. Loening.

Wilkins, F. H. *Early Influence of German Literature in America.* Appendix contains list of German works printed in America before 1826. N. Y. MacMillan, 1899. 105 pp. (Also printed in Americana-Germanica Series, III: 103-126.)

B.—Goethe's Works In Sets 1. *Bohn's Standard Library" Goethe's Works.* First volume, *Goethe's Dramatic Works,* published by Bohn, Lond., 1847. Taken over by George Bell & Co. in 1864.

Latest edition, 14 vols, in 1908. Bell & Co. Lond.; Mac millan Co. N. Y. Vol. VII. *Goethe's Poems and Ballads,* by E. A.

Bowring, added in 1874.

CONTENTS TRANSLATOR DATE
Vol. I, II.

Autobiography, (Poetry and Truth from my Life) John Oxenford 1848

Revised translation Minna Steele Smith 1904

Vol. III.

Faust, first part Anna Swanwick 1850
Faust, second part Anna Swanwick 1879
Vol. IV.

Novels and Tales:

Elective Affinities, Good Women, Werter, German Emigrants, Nouvellette, A Fairy Tale R. D. Boylan 1854

Vol. V.

Wilhelm Meister's Apprenticeship R. D. Boylan 1855
» Goedeke's *Grundriss,* (3. Aufiage, 4. Band, 3. Abteilung, 1. Heft, §34) mentions this edition as appearing in 1846, and includes Bowring's volume of poems. Upon investigation I find that the *Bohn Library* was not begun until 1847. George Bell & Sons, who took over the *Bohn Library* in 1864, write me that no volume of poems was included at that time. In the book lists and catalogs of the time there is no record of the incorporation of these poems in the set previous to 1874, and then Bowring's translation of 1853 was added.

Goedeke's *Grundriss* also states that previous to 1876 three editions of Goethe's works, (presumably poems also), appeared in the United States: viz. , Appleton, N. T. 6 vols. 12; Lippincott, Phila. 7 vols. 12; Bohn, Boston and N. T. 7 vols. 12. Letters from these various publishing houses state that they have no records of these publications and cannot tell whether any of them appeared before 1860 or not, nor do they know whether these were all copies of the Bohn translations. Bell & Co. write, "We have no doubt that the American editions had been reprinted from Bohn without acknowledgement."

Vol. VI.

Conversations with Soret and Eckermann

Vol. VII.

Goethe's Poems and Ballads (including *Hermann und Dorothea*)

Vol. VIII.

Gotz von Berlichingen....
Tasso, Egmont
Iphigenia
Clavigo, The Wayward Lov-

er, *The Fellow Culprits.*
Vol. IX.
Wilhelm Meister's Travels.
Vol. X.
Travels in Italy and *Second
Residence in Rome*
    Vol. XI.
    Miscellaneous Travels of
Goethe: *Letters from
Switzerland, The Cam-
paign in France, The
Siege of Mainz, The Tour
on the Rhine*
    Vol. XII.
    Early and miscellaneous
Letters, including letters
to his mother
    Vol. XIII.
Correspondence with Zelter.
(out of print)
    Vol. XIV.
*Reineke Fox, West-East-
erly Divan, Achilleid....
(Correspondence with Schil-
ler,* printed by the *Bohn
Library* but not included in the regular
set.)
    John Oxenford 1850
    E. A. Bowring 1853
    Walter Scott 1799
    Anna Swanwick 1850
    Anna Swanwick 1843
    E. A. Bowring 1879
    Edward Bell 1882
    A. J. W. Morrison 1849
    Dora Schmitz 1882
    Edward Bell 1884
    A. D. Coleridge 1877
    Alex. Rogers 1890
    Dora Schmitz 1877
2. *The Works of Goethe.* Edited and revised by F. H. Hedge and L. Noa.
(a) People's Edition. 9 vols. 8. S. E.
Cassino.
1882. Bost.
(b) People's Edition. 9 vols, in 5. 12.
Estes &
Lauriat. 1882. Bost.
(c) People's Edition. 9 vols, in 5. 12.
Crowell &
Co. 1882. N. Y.
(d) People's Edition. Same as above.
Bost, and N.
Y. 1885.
(e) Universal Edition. 5 vols. 12. S. E.

Cassino. 1885. Bost.
(f) Goethe's Popular Works. Edited by
Hedge and Noa. Cambridge Edition. 10
vols. 12. Cassino, Bost.; Crowell, N. Y.,
1882. Identical with (a). (g) Cambridge
Edition. 10 vols. Cambridge, Mass.
1895. Same as (a) and (f).
    Vol. VI in this first edition and the
corresponding volume in the other editions contains Goethe's poems, the
"eclectic volume". It is constituted as
follows: 274 poems by Bowring, 68 by
Aytoun-Martin, 5 by Noa, 2 by Lewes,
3 by Chawner, 2 by Dwight, 1 each by
Longfellow, Carlyle, Bayard Taylor,
Sprague, Dale, Morrison. For exact contents see Bibliography C, footnote 72.
All the other works in these editions
are the same as those used in the *Bohn
Library,* except *Wilhelm Meister,* which
is here found in Carlyle's translation,
while Bohn uses that of R. D. Boylan.
3. *The Works of Johann Wolfgang von
Goethe.* Gottingen
Edition. With an introduction by
Thomas Carlyle, and with photogravure
plates on Japan paper, including the celebrated Goethe Gallery of William von
Kaulbach. Translated by Henry W.
Longfellow, Thomas Carlyle, Sir Walter Scott, Bayard Taylor, Anna Swanwick, and others. 10 vols. 8. J. H. Moore
& Co. Phil, and Chic. 1882. 2nd edition,
Phil, and Chic. 1901. Vol. V, *Poems of
Goethe,* eclectic volume, same as 2. All
other works identical with *Bohn's Library,* except that to Swanwick's translation of *Faust* has been added the prose
translation of part I, by A. Hayward.
4. *Goethe's Works,* with Life by Hjalmar
Boyesen. Beauti fully printed and very
richly illustrated. 5 vols. Large quarto.
(Life, pp. 3-34.) Barrie, Phil. 1885.
"Goedeke's *Orvndriss* 5235, p. 35,
mentions this edition as being by H.
Boyesen and therefore ascribes all the
translations In it to Boyesen, whereas
really only 31 pages of the introduction
are his work. E. Os
    Vol. I, *Goethe's Poems* is the eclectic
volume, as in the other American editions, except that to this have been
added a few epigrams, 7 elegies in
Martin's translation, and 15 sonnets.
The other works are identical with

Bohn's Library, no. 1 (except *Rey-
nard the Fox,* given in the translation of
T. J.
Arnold.)
    In none of the five volumes are the
names of any translators given. The only name mentioned in connection with
the set is that of Boyesen, which has led
to some bibliographical errors.
5. *The Life and Works of Goethe.* Selected. 6 vols. Quarto.
Houghton & Mifflin, Bost., 1885.
No Poems; vol. I, *Goethe's Life* by G. H.
Lewes; vol. II
and III, *Faust* by Bayard Taylor; vol. IV,
*Goethe's
Correspondence with a Child;* vols. V
and VI, *Wil-
helm Meister* by Carlyle.
6. *The Works of Johann Wolfgang von
Goethe.* Edition de
luxe, with portraits and plates.
Amaranth Society,
London. 10 vols. 1901. Also published
in Phil, and
Chicago. This seems to be entirely iden-
tical with the Gottingen Edition pub-
lished by J. H. Moore &
Co. in 1882 and 1901.
    Vol. V, *The Poems of Goethe,* is the
eclectic volume.
Other works are the same as the Bohn
edition.
    The title page says, "Translated by
Henry W. Longfellow, Thomas Carlyle,
Sir Walter Scott, Bayard Taylor, Anna
Swanwick and others." Longfellow
translated, of the ten volumes, the two
*Wanderer's Night
Songs,* (sixteen short lines); Carlyle
translated the
Wilhelm Meister; Scott, the *Gotz;* Bayard Taylor,
the *King of Thule,* (twenty-four lines);
his translation of *Faust* was not used but
rather that of
Swanwick; also Swanwick's translation
of *Iphi-
genia, Egmont,* and *Tasso.* Otherwise
the ten
wald in his bibliography, *Goethe t»
England and America,* makes the same
error, for example, Scott's *Gdtz,* Swanwick's *Egmont,* and both parts of *Faust,*
Bowrlng's *Clavigo* and *Hermann and*

Dorothea are all attributed to Boyesen. volumes are the work of translators whose names are not mentioned. 7. (a) *Goethe's Works.* Weimar Edition. Edited by N. H.

Dole. Translated by Samuel Taylor Coleridge, John

Storer Cobb, Anna Swanwick and others. 14 vols.

8. Limited to 1000 copies. F. A. Niccolls & Co.

Bost. 1902.

Vol. IX, *Poems of Goethe,* eclectic volume. *Goethe's Life*

by G. H. Lewes, *Wilhelm Meister by* Carlyle, *Faust,*

part I, by Theodore Martin, otherwise the *Bohn*

translations are given. In spite of the title page,

an examination of the contents fails to show any translations by Coleridge, and only *The Reineke Fox*

by Cobb.

(b) *Goethe's Works,* Lyceum Edition. 14 vols. Limited to 750 copies. F. A. Niccolls Co. Bost. 1912.

Vol. IX, eclectic volume of poems. Other works like (a).

(c) *Goethe's Works.* Edited by N. H. Dole. 7 vols.

International Publ. Co. N. Y. 1902. Vol. I, Poems,

eclectic volume. Other works like (a).

(d) *Goethe's Poetical Works.* Edited by N. H. Dole.

Translated by Samuel Taylor Coleridge, John

Storer Cobb, Anna Swanwick and others. 2 vols.

F. A. Niccolls Co. Bost. 1902.

Contains no poems, *Faust,* two parts, by Theodore Martin, *Egmont* by Swanwick, *Clavigo* and *Wayward*

Lover by Bowring. nothing translated by Coleridge.

The Francis A. Niccolls Co. of Boston write me that they have sold the rights to these translations to other firms for cheap trade editions, the contents of the latter being of course identical with edition 7 (a). So it is very probable that there are other editions of Goethe's works in circulation, which I have not happened to find, and which are not in-

cluded here. But it is not probable that any of them offer anything new in the way of translations.

Goedeke's *Grundriss,* 1235, p. 35. mentions this edition but not accurately, evidently confusing it with the seven volume edition.

C.—Single Volumes Of Goethe's Poems 1. *Select Minor Poems of Goethe and Schiller.* With notes by Jonathan S. Dwight. Edited by George Ripley as vol. III of the series, *Specimens of Foreign Standard Literature.* Hilliard, Gray & Co., Boston. 1839. pp. XX and 439. 16. (,pp. 1-197, Goethe, 85 poems.) Reviewed in: *B. Quart.* 1839. II:187;. *B. Christ. Exam.* 1839, XXVI: 360; 1840, XXIX: 117; *Dub. Univ. Mag.* 1844, XXIV: 379; *Knickerbocker,* N. Y. 1851, XXXVII: 358; *Ladies' Repository,* Cinn. 1841. I:127; *N. Amer. Rev.* 1839, XLVII:505; *N. Y. Rev.* 1839, IV: 393; *West. Mess.* 1839, VI: 259. Contents: Translated by Bancroft; *Joy, Salutation of a Spirit, My Goddess, The Divine, Cupid as Landscape Painter.*

By W. H. Channing, *Mignon.*

By J. F. Clarke, *For Life, For Ever, Orphic Sayings. In Memory of Schiller-Epilogue to Schiller's Bell.*

By N. L. Frothingham, *Song of the Fates from Iphigenia, Stability in Change.* There might well be included here the following volume; *Goethe's Poetical Works* (or *Poems of Goethe).* In the original metres, by Bowring, Lewes, Carlyle, Longfellow, and others. Crowell & Co. N. T. 1882. pp. 439.

This has been referred to throughout this investigation as the eclectic volume. Nearly all the translations in it were made before 1860. It is the one most generally known in this country; as can be seen from Bibliography *B,* it is the collection of poems used by all the publishers, except Bohn. who have presented Goethe's works in sets.

Contents: Bowring, (1853), 274 poems; Aytoun-Martin, (1844-1859). 68 poems; Dwight, (1839), 2 poems, *To the Moon, The Harz Mountains;* Lewes, (1855), 2 poems, *From the Mountain, The Fisher;* Longfellow. (1845), 1 poem, *Wanderer's Night Song;* Carlyle. (1824), 1 poem, *Mignon;* Dale, (1859),

1 poem, *Hermann and Dorothea;* Morrison. (1850), 1 poem, *To Belinda;* Chawner, (1866), 3 poems. *Spirit Greeting, Vanitas. nance of the Dead;* Bayard Taylor, (1870), 1 poem, *The King of Thule;* Sprague, (1870), 1 poem,. *Song of the Spirits over the Waters:* Noa, (1876), 5 poems, On *the Lake, To a Golden Heart, Delight of Sorrow, Ballad of the Exiled Count, Legend of the Horseshoe.*

By Margaret Fuller, *To a Golden Heart, Eagles and Doves (sic).*

By G. W. Haven, *(from Faust) The Song of the Angels, Gretchen's Song. By F. H. Hedge, The Erlking.*

By Dwight, see Bibliography F, 61 poems, besides parables, epigrams and proverbs.

2. *Poems of Goethe.'* Translated in the original metres, with a sketch of Goethe's life. Edward Alfred Bowring. Parker, Lond. 1853. pp. 433. 8. Edition revised by the author in 1874. *Hermann and Dorothea* and more translations from the *West-Eastern Divan* added, as vol. VII of *Bohn's Standard Library.* Lond. Bell.

Reviewed in: *L. Athen.* 1853, No. 1358, p. 1319; *L. Examiner,* 1853; Littell's *Living Age,* 1853, XXXVIII: 123.

3. *Poems and Ballads of Goethe,* with notes, by W. E. Ay toun and Sir Theodore Martin. Blackwood's. Lond. and Edin. 1859. Delisser & Proctor, N. Y. 1859. pp. xv and 240. 8. Last edition. Lond. and Edin. Blackwood's. 1908. Reviewed in: *L. Athen.* 1859, p. 215; *Bentley's Misc.* 1859, XLV: 401; *Brit. Quart. Rev.* 1859, XXIX: 550; *Eclect. Mag. B.* 1860, XIIX: 53; *Fraser's Mag.* 1859, LIX: 710; *Lit. World,* B. 1871, II: 91; Littell's *Liv. Age,* B. 1859, LXI:181; *L. Quart. Rev.* 1859, XII: 121; *L. Sat. Rev.* 1859, VII: 187; VIII: 456; *North Brit. Rev.* 1859, XXX: 270; *Once a Week,* L. 1859, I: 89; *Scottish Rev. Edin.* 1859, p. 199; *Overland Mo.* San Francisco. 1872, VIII: 200; *Southern Mag.* Balt. 1871. XIX: 755. 4. *Minor Poetry of Goethe.* A Selection of Songs and Ballads and Lesser Poems. "William Grassett Thomas. Phil. Butler & Co. 1859. pp. xxxiv and 335. 8. TM See footnote

47. See footnotes 51 and 52.

D.—List Of Anthologies And Other Books, Containing Translations From Goethe

1. *Specimens of German Lyric Poets.* (Beresford.) See no. 9 below. 1798 (?)

2. *German Erato.* A collection of favorite songs translated into English with original music by Reichardt. The translator is the author of *Specimens of German Lyrics.* Berlin. C. Falk. 1798. pp. 31. (Sold in London by Boosey). In one catalogue this was listed as a second edition.

Mention is made of this book in the *Brit. Critic,* 1799, XIII: 694; *Poetical Mag.* Lond. 1801, I: 386; *Mo. Mirror,* 1802, XIV: 402; *Mo. Register,* Lond. 1803, II: 333; *Lond. Poet. Register,* 1804, IV: 446; V: 218; *L. Mo. Review,* 1805, XL: 75; *Westminster Rev.,* 1824, I:557.

Contains poems 75, 103, 104, 105, 108.

3. *German Songster,* or a collection of favorite airs with their original music, done into English by the translator of the *German Erato.* Berlin. C. Falk. 1798. pp. 27. 4. 2nd Edition, Berlin, Frohlich. 1800. (Sold in London by Boosey.) Reviewed by the same magazines as no. 2. Contains 75, 103,104, 105, 108.

4. *A Collection of German Ballads and Songs,* with their original music done into English by the translator of the *German Erato.* Berlin, 2nd Edit. Frohlich. 1800. pp. 32. 4. Contains 104, 108.

An asterisk marks those books which are mentioned as containing translations from Goethe, but which I have not been able to examine and verify.

The titles are arranged chronologically, and the individual poems found in the various volumes are indicated by the number they have In the subsequent list, E.

5. *German Museum* or Monthly Repository of the Literature of Germany, the North, and the Continent in General. Nov. to Dec. 1800; Jan. to June, 1801. With numerous sheets of music by Mozart, Reichart, Weisse, and translated poems of Goethe. L. Geisweiler. 2 vols. 1800-1801. Royal 8.

Reviewed in the *Brit. Critic,* XVII: 669, 1801.

Contains 165 and others not verified.

6. *Tales of Wonder.* Matthew Gregory Lewis. Lond. Bell, 1801. N. Y. Nicholas, 1801. (Reprinted, Lond. Routledge, 1887.) Contains 106, 107, 108, 370. 7. *Translations from German Miscellaneous Poetry.* W. Herbert. L. Reynolds. 1804. Rev. in the *Brit. Critic,* 1804, XXV: 138; *L. Mo. Mag.* 1804, XIV: 75.

8. *Lays of a Wanderer.* A series of songs in English with music by C. Walter. L. Johanning & Whatmore. 1820. Folio. Contains 37,104.

9. *Specimens of German Lyric Poets,* translated into verse from Burger, Goethe, Klopstock, Schiller. (Beresford.) Lond. Boosey, 1821. pp. 152. 8. 2nd edit. 1822. (Preface says, "The chief portion of these were published twenty years ago at Berlin, with musical melodies. The words were translated by an English gentleman, Beresford, a few were added by Mr. Mellish, late British consul at Hamburg.") It is sometimes cataloged as the "Beresford-Mellish Lyrics." 3rd edit. Blackwood's 1823. 4th edit. Longman's. 1828. Rev. in *Bost. Quart. Rev.,* 1821, XXV: 276; 1822, XXVII: 559; *Amer. Meth. Mag.,* 1822, XI: 114; *Blackwood's Mag.,* 1822, II: 172; *European Mag.,* 1822, LXXXI:156; *Athenaeum,* B. 1822, XI: 144; *Athenaeum,* L. 1828, I: 500; *Museum of Foreign Lit.* Phil., 1828, XIII: 15.

Contains 74, 75, 103, 104, 105, 108, 109.

10. *Life and Genius of Goethe.* George Bancroft. B. Everett, pp. 24, 8. First printed as an essay in *N. Amer.Rev.* 1824, XIX: 303-325. Bost. Contains 41, 69, 103, 105, 108, 110, 167, 172.

11. *Translations from the German and Original Poems.* Lord Francis Leveson Gower, (Francis Egerton, Earl of Ellesmere.) Lond. Murray, 1824. pp. 153. 8.

Reviewed in *L. Lit. Gazette,* 1824; *Westminster Rev.,* 1824, I; *Western Rev.,* 1824, I; *Edin. Rev.,* 1830, LII: 231; *Dublin Rev.,* XIX.

Contains 110.

12. *Cabinet of Poetry and Romance.* Robinson. Lond. 1825.

Contains 107.

13. *Torquato Tasso.* A dramatic poem from the German of Goethe and other German poetry from Goethe, Schiller, Burger, Eichendorf, Holty, and Uhland. By Charles Des Voeux. Lond. Longmans, 1827. pp. 307. 8. 2nd edit. Weimar, 1833. Reviewed in *L. Lit. Gazette,* 1827, VI: 182; *L. Mo. Rev.,* 1827, VII: 453.

Contains 34, 37, 49, 63, 64, 72, 75, 104, 105, 107, 109, 110, 129, 189, 300, 367, 373.

14. *Stray Leaves,* including translations from the lyric poets of Germany, with brief notices of their lives. Lond. Treuttel. Edin. Clark, 1827. pp. 165. 12. Reviewed in *L. Mirror,* 1827, X: 144; *L. Mo. Rev.,* 1827, VI:126.

15. *Employment.* Frederick Page. Bath, Eng., Upham, 1828. Pamphlet, pp. 44. 8. Contains 37, 228, 375.

16. *Specimens of the German Lyric Poets,* by Robert Robinson of Dukinfeld. Lond. Longmans, 1828. pp. 110. 8.

Reviewed in *L. Athenaeum,* I:500. Contains 32, 37, 39, 40, 74, 103, 325.

17. *Golden Lyre.* Specimens of the

Poets of England, France, Germany, Italy and Spain. Edited by John Macray, Lond. 1829. Rev. in *Edin. Lit. Jour.,* 1829, II:307; *New Mo. Mag.* Lond. 1829, XXVII: 12; *L. Ath.* 1830, III: 135.

18. *Historic Survey of German Poetry.* William Taylor of Norwich. 3 vols. Lond. Treuttel & Wurtz. 1st vol. 1828. 3rd vol. includes Goethe, 1830. pp. 506. 8.

Reviewed in *Edin. Rev.,* 1831, LIII: 151; (Same article in Carlyle's *Essays,* III: 217); *Amer. Quart. Rev.,* 1830, VII: 436; 1831, X:194.

Contains 103, 104, 107, 108, 109, 127, 128, 133, 142, 165, 224, 368, 380, 381.

19. *Characteristics of Goethe,* from the German of Falk, von Miiller, and others, with notes original and translated, illustrative of German Literature, by Sarah Austin. Lond. Wilson. 1833. 3 vols. 8. Later edit., Wilson, Lond. 1836, called *Goethe and His Contemporaries.* Phil. Lea & Blanchard, 1841.

Reviewed in *Amer. Meth. Mag.,* N. Y. 1833, XXIII: 500; *Dublin Univ. Mag.,* 1836, VIII: 350; *Edin. Rev.,* 1833, LVII; *Gentlemen's Mag.* 1833, CI-II:137; *L. Mo. Rev.* 1833, CXXXI; *Museum of For. Lit.* Phil. 1833, XXIII: 500; *North Amer. Rev.* 1833, II: 289; *Select Jour. of For. Lit. Bost.,* 1833, I: 923; II: 289.

Contains 73, 93, 95, 136, 138, 139, 142,173,179, 288, 362.

20. *The Literary Rambler.* A Collection of the Most Popular and Entertaining Stories in the English Language. Edinburg. 1833. Contains 24, 65, 295.

21. *Lays and Legends of Germany.* W. J. Thorns. Lond.

Cowie, 1834. Reviewed in *L. Ath.* VII: 222.

22. *Flowers of German Poetry.* J. G. Fligel. Lond. 1835. Contains 371.

23. *Anthologia Germanica.* J. Clarence Mangan. *Dublin Univ. Mag.* 1835-1846, vols. V-XIV and XVIII-XXVII. (Goethe vols. V, VII, IX.) Contains 6, 69, 91, 92, 93, 103, 104, 105, 107, 108, 109, 110, 113, 164, 233, 236, 323, 372, 378.

24. *German Wreath.* Translations in poetry and prose from celebrated German writers, with biographies and explanatory notes, by Hermann Bokum, instructor in German at Harvard Univ. Bost..Munroe, 1836. pp. 146. 12.

Reviewed in *N. Amer. Rev.* XLII: 556. 1836. Contains 41, 75, 103, 104, 107, 108, 109, 127, 224.

25. *Song of the Bell* and other Poems from the German of Goethe, Schiller, Burger, Mathisson and Salis. John J. Campbell. Edin. Blackwood, 1836. pp. 259. Contains 6, 23, 37, 50, 64, 85, 88, 97, 102, 103, 109, 110, 128, 196, 298, 371.

26. *Library of Romance.* A Collection of Traditions, Poetical Legends and Short Standard Tales of All Nations. Lond. 1836. Contains 107, 125.

27. *Goethe's Correspondence with a Child,* Bettina von Arnim. Translated into English by herself and Mrs. Sarah Austin. Lond. Longmans, 1837. pp. 540. Lowell, Mass. Bixby. 1840. Boston, Ticknor & Fields. 1859.

Reviewed in *Atl. Mo.* 1860, V:251; 1873, XXXI: 210; *Blackwood's Mag.* 1845, IX; *B. Dial,* 1841, II: 134; *Jour. of Books,* N. Y. 1841, I: 255; *L. Ath.* 1839, p.

169; *Lond. Mo. Rev.* 1840, p. 144; *Nat'l Quart. Rev.* Lond. 1871, no. 41; *New Englander,* 1860, XVIII: 549; *Russell's Mag.* 1860, VI: 382; *Tait's Edin. Mag.* 1842, IX.

Contains 72, 144, 147, 148, 150, 151, 152, 153, 159, 358.

28. *Translations from the Lyric Poets of Germany,* with brief notices of their lives and writings. John Macray. Lond. Blackwoods. 1838. 8. Reviewed in *L. Ath.* 1838, p. 728; *L. Spectator,* 1838, XI: 519; *Dub. Univ. Mag.* 1839, XIII: 643; *L. Mirror,* 1840, XXXVI: 90.

29. *Capuciner.* N. Y. Radde. 1839. pp. 23. 16. Contains 108, 110. 30. *Life and Correspondence of M. G. Lewis.* Lond. Colburn, 2 vols. 1839. Contains 105.

31. *A Drama and Other Poems.* S. Naylor. Maidenhead, Eng. 1839. pp. 166. Contains 89, 226, 372.

32. *Poems.* Robert Fraser. Poetical Remains with a Memoir of the Author, by D. Vedder. Lond. 1839. 8. Contains 3, 14, 93. 33. *The Drama of Life.* J. E. Reade. L. Saunders & Otley. 1840. pp. 162. 8.

Reviewed in *L. Mo. Chronicle,* 1839. IV: 405.

Contains 103, 372, 377, 379, 381.

34. *Specimens of German Lyrical Poetry.* Illustrations of German Poetry with notes. Elijah Barwell Impey. Lond. Simpkins. 1841. 2 vols. 12.

Reviewed in *Dub. Univ. Mag.* 1842, XIX: 330; *L. Lit. Gazette,* 1841, p. 105.

Contains 127.

35. *Ballads, Songs and, Poems,* translated from the German. Lord Lindsay. Lond. C. Sims. 1841. pp. 159. Folio.

Contains 71, 107,108,109.

36. *Design and Border Illustrations* to poems from Goethe, Schiller, Uhland, Burger, etc. with translations. J. B. Sunderland. Lond. Senior. 1841. pp. 30. Folio.

Reviewed in *Christ. Remembrancer,*

1841. II: 395; *Dub. Univ. Mag.* 1841. XIX: 331.
Contains 114, 127.
37. *Ideals and Other Poems.* "Algernon. " Phil. Perkins.
1842. pp. 102. Contains 23, 372, 384.
38. *Songs and Ballads,* translated from Goethe, Schiller (and from fifteen other German lyric poets) with notes. Chas. T. Brooks. Bost. Munroe, Lond. Green. 1842. pp. 360. Reviewed in *Amer. Bibl. Repository,* 1842, series 2, VIII: 479; *Christ. Rev.,* 1842, VII: 626; *Knickerbocker,* 1842, XX: 484; *B. Mo. Misc.* 1842, VII: 290; *Christ. Exam.* Bost. 1843, XXXIV: 232. Contains 39, 103, 107, 108, 137. 39. *The New Hampshire Book,* Specimens of Lit. Edited by Chas. J. Fox and Sam'l Osgood. Nashua, N. H., Marshall. Bost. Munroe. 1842. pp. 391. 16. Contains 372.
40. *Translations from German Prose and Verse.* H. Reeve and J. E. Taylor. Lond. Murray. 1842, pp. 78. Contains 384. 41. *Goethe's Poems and Ballads.* Essay with translations, (Aytoun and Martin) *Blackwood's Mag.* 1844, LVI:54; 1845, LVII:165. Reviewed in *Fraser's Mag.* Lond. 1859, LIX: 710; *Eclectic Mag.* Bost. 1860, XLV: 53; *L. Quart. Rev.* 1859, XII: 121. Contains 1, 6, 22, 30, 35, 37, 38, 45, 46, 49, 50, 64, 68, 70, 71, 72, 103, 104, 105, 107, 108, 109, 110, 113, 125, 127, 128, 129, 164, 173, 189, 198, 199, 201, 203, 204, 205, 206, 207, 208, 209, 210, 211, 212, 213, 214, 215, 217, 218, 219, 220, 221, 225, 226, 369, 370. 42. *Poems,* Original and Translated. Dedicated to Joanna Baillie, by John Hermann Merivale. Lond. Pickering. 1844. 3 vols. Contains 37, 44, 92, 127, 372.
43. *German Ballads and Songs.* Edited by James Burns. Translated from Goethe, Schiller, etc. Lond. Robison. 1845. pp. 200. Reviewed in *Gentleman's Mag.* 1845, XXIV: 509; *Tail's Edin. Mag.* 1846, XIII: 94.
Contains 103,104.
44. *Critical and Miscellaneous Essays.* A. H. Everett. Bost. Munroe. 1845. Contains 371, 375.
45. *Poems,* Original and Translated. A.

H. Everett. Bost. Munroe. 1845. pp. 410. 12.
Contains 371, 375.
46. *The Spirit of German Poetry,* with translations and bio graphical notes. Joseph Gostick (Gostwick). Lond. Smith, 1845. 8.
Reviewed in *L. AtJi.* 1845, p. 1242; *J err old's Shilling Mag.* Lond. 1846. III:84.
Contains 13, 68, 103, 109, 229, 372, 383, 384.
47. *The Poets and Poetry of Europe.* Edited by Henry W. Longfellow. Phil. Porter & Coates. Lond. Chapman. 1845. pp. 916. 8. Reviewed in *Amer. Whig Rev.* 1846, IV: 580; *Christ. Exam.* 1845, XXXIX: 225; *Dem. Rev.* 1846, XX: 121; *N. Am. Rev.* 1845, LXI: 199. Contains 37, 64, 69, 72, 73, 75, 93, 165, 166, 173, 371, 380, 381, 383.
48. *German Anthology,* A Garland from the German Poets.
James Clarence Mangan. Dublin, Curry & Co.
1845. 2 vols. pp. 206, 203. (N. Y. Haverty, 1859.) Reviewed in *Brit. Quart. Rev.* 1845, II: 582; *Dub. Rev.* 1845, XIX: 312; *Eng. Rev.* 1845, IV: 222; *For. Quart. Rev.* 1845, XXXVI: 238; *L. Spectator,* 1846, XIX: 1003; *Tait's Edin. Mag.* 1846, XIII: 94. Contains 6, 69, 91, 92, 93,103,104, 105, 107,108, 109, 110, 113, 164, 233, 236. 49. *Translations from Goethe.* "P. M." *Blackwood's Mag.*
,
Edin. LIX:120. 1846.
Contains 131, 202, 205, 221.
50. *The Diadem for MDCCCXLVI.* A Present for All Seasons, Translated from Goethe, Schiller, Uhland, Richter, and Zschokke. Phil. Carey & Hunt. 1846.
pp. 95.
Contains 107.
51. *Wild Flowers.* A Collection of Gems from the Best Authors. Miss Colman. Bost. Colman. 1846.
pp. 126. 24. Reissued 1848 as *Ladies' Vase of Wild Flowers.*
52. *English Hexameter Translations* from Schiller, Goethe,

Homer, Callinus, and Meleager. (J. C. Hare?)
Lond. Murray, 1847. pp. 277. 8. Reviewed in
L. Lit. Gaz. 1847. pp. 277.
Contains 137, 139.
53. *Prose and Poetry of Europe and America.* Compiled by G. P. Morris and N. P. Willis. N. Y. Leavitt, Trow & Co. 1847. pp. 598.
Contains 383.
54. *Book of Ballads from the German.* Percy Boyd, Esq. Dublin, Orr. 1848. 8.
Reviewed in *L. Ath.* 1848, p. 458; *Dub. Univ. Mag.* 1848. XXXI: 305; *Westm. Rev.* XLIX: 261.
Contains 112.
55. *A Collection of Select Pieces of Poetry,* by Schiller and Burger, together with some characteristic poems of the most eminent German bards. Translated in the meters of the originals. George Ph. Maurer. N. Y. Lange. 1848. pp. 141. 16.
Contains 45, 46, 107.
56. *The Beauties of German Literature.* J. Burns. Lond. 1849. 12.
57. *First General History of German Literature.* J. Gostick (Gostwick.) Edin. 1849. pp. 324. Phil. Lippincott, 1854.
Contains 383, 384, and many short selections and fragments of Goethe's verse.
58. *Schiller's Song of the Bell.* A New Translation by "W. H." Furness, with Poems and Ballads from Goethe, Schiller and others, by F. H. Hedge. Phil. Hazard.
1850. pp. 48. 16. Reviewed in *Knickerbocker,* 1851. XXXVII: 357. Contains 69,104, 108, 372.
59. *Poems and Translations from the German* of Goethe, Schiller, Chamisso, Uhland, Riickert, etc. C. R. Lambert. Lond. Whitaker & Co. 1850. (Goethe, pp. 81-98).
   Reviewed in *Russell's Mag.* 1859, V: 93.
Contains 23, 37, 41,108, 109, 123, 360, 372.

60. *Memoirs of a Literary Veteran.* R. P. Gillies. Lond.
Bentley, 3 vols. 1851.
Contains 384.

61. *Metrical Translations from thi German,* (Goethe, Schiller,
Uhland, Heine), by a German Lady, (Mrs. Adela Haller.) Lond. Williams & Norgate. 1852. pp. 167. 8. Also published in Hamburg. Contains 6, 11, 20, 63, 64, 69, 70, 71, 72, 73, 74, 75, 103, 104, 105, 108, 109, 173, 181, 195, 198, 365, 368, 371, 378.

62. *The Poetry of Germany,* consisting of selections from upwards of seventy of the most celebrated poets, translated into English verse with the original text on the opposite page. Alfred Baskerville. Leipzig, Mayer; N. Y. Garrigue; Lond. "Williams & Norgate, 1853. pp. 332. 8. (14th Edit. Phil. Schaefer & Koradi, 1886). Reviewed in *L. Ath.* 1854, p. 1427; *Christ. Exam.* Bost. 1854, LVII: 464; *Harper's Mo. Mag.* IX: 857; *Putnam's Mag.* 1854, IV: 562; *Littell's Liv. Age,* 1855, LXIV: 548; *MetJi. Quart. Rev.* 1855, XV: 137. Contains 6, 9, 10, 13, 14, 45, 46, 49, 50, 52, 60, 63, 64, 75, 85, 103, 104 105, 107, 108, 113, 122, 130. 63. *Gems of German Verse,* from Goethe, Schiller, Uhland,
Heine, Korner, edited by Wm, H. Furness. Illustrations by Retzsch. Phil. Hazard. 1853. pp. 150.
16. Revised and enlarged, 1860.
Reviewed in *Lit. World,* N. Y. 1853, XII: 43; *Norton's Lit. Gaz.* 1852, III:20; *CJir. Exam.* 1860, LXVIII: 311.
Contains 69, 104, 107, 372.

64. *Thalatta,* A Book for the Seaside. Compiled by Samuel
Longfellow and Thos. W. Higginson. Bost. Ticknor, 1853. pp. 206. 16. Contains 108.

65. *Hours of Life and Other Poems,* translated from the Ger man. Sarah Helen Whitman. Prov. R. I. Whitney. 1853. Reviewed in *Christ. Exam.* 1855, XX: 39. Contains 383. 66. *Specimens of the Choicest Lyrical Productions* of the most celebrated German poets, from Klopstock to the present time, with biographies and literary notices. Mary

Anne Burt. Leipzig, 1854; Lond. Hall, 1856, pp.
504.
Reviewed in *Lond. Lit. Gazette.* 1855, p. 649.
Contains 1, 2, 3, 4, 5, 6, 7, 8, 9, 10, 12, 13, 14, 15, 16, 17,
18,19, 20,103,104,107, 110,126, 164.

67. *Literary and. Historic Miscellanies.* George Bancroft.
N. Y. Harper. 1855. pp. 517.
Contains 41, 69, 105,110,164,167,176.

68. *Metrical Pieces,* Translated and Original, from Goethe,
Schiller, Herder, R. Riickert, Uhland, Auersperg, etc. N. L. Frothingham. Bost. Crosby & Nicholls.
1855. pp. 362. 16. Reviewed in *LitteU's Liv. Age.* 1856, L:24. Contains 86, 368.
69. *Gleanings from the Poets.* Bost. Crosby & Nichols. 1855. New edit. 70. *Torquato Tasso and Other Poems,* translated and original, with extracts from Goethe, Schiller, Korner, Uhland, Kosegarten, Mathisson. "M. A. H." Lond. Longmans. 12. 2nd edit. 1856. Reviewed in *L. Ath.* 1857. p. 498. 71. *Echoes of Leisure Hours with the German Poets.* Asahel
C. Kendrick. Rochester, N. Y. Sage; N. Y. Evans & Dickersonj Chic. Griggs, 1855. pp. 148. 16.
Reviewed in *Christ. Rev.* 1855, XX: 636; *Norton's Literary Gazette.* 1855, II:153; *West. Lit. Mess.* XXIV: 17.
Contains 107, 110, 127.

72. *Poetry and Mystery of Dreams.* Chas. G. Leland, ("Hans Breitmann".) Containing translations from Goethe, Schiller, Heine, Uhland, Richter, Gerstenberg, etc.
Phil. Butler & Co. 1855. pp. 270. 12. Contains 108.

73. *Life and Works of Goethe* with sketches of his age and con temporaries, from published and unpublished sources.
George Henry Lewes. Lond. Nutt. 1855. 2 vols,
pp. 786. 8; Bost. Ticknor, 1856. 2 vols. pp. 945.
12. 2nd edit. Lond. Smith. 1864, partly rewritten. 4th edit. 1890. Everyman's Lib. Lond. Dent.
1908.

Reviewed in 1855, in Eng., *Fras. Mag.* LII: 639; *L. Lit.*
Gaz. p. 691; *L. Sped.* XVIII: 113; in 1856, in
Eng., *Bentley's Misc.* Lond. XXXIX: 96; *Brit.*
Quart. Rev. XXXIII: 468; *Eel. Rev.* Lond. CIV: 447;
New Quart. Rev. V: 11; *Sat. Rev.* I: 99; *Tait's Edin.*
Mag. XXIII: 136; in 1856, in Amer., *Christ. Rev.*
XXI: 412; *Criterion,* N. Y. I:164; *Dem. Rev.*
XXXVII: 157; *Eel. Mag.* XXXVII:200; *Graham's*
Mag. XLVIII:439; *Knickerbocker,* XLVII:187;
LitteU's Liv. Age. XLVIII: 91; L: 1; *N. Am. Rev.*
LXXXII: 564; *Panorama of Life and Lit.* Bost.
II: 332; *Putnam's Mag.* VII: 104,192; *S. Lit. Mess.*
XXII: 160.
Contains 50, 51, 57, 108, 132, 173, 367, 377.

74. *Legends and Ballads from the German.* J. C. D. Huber.
'Lond. Whittaker. 1856. 12.

75. *Lyrical Poems from the German.* J. E. Reade. Lond.
Longmans. 1856.

76. *The German Lyrist.* Translations from Klopstock,
Goethe, Schiller, Burger, etc. ¥m. Nind. Lond.
Bell & Daldy. 1856. 8. Reviewed in *N. Y. World.*
1856, XV: 229; *L. Ath.* 1857, p. 499.

77. *The Household Book of Poetry.* Edited by Chas. A. Dana.
N. Y. Appleton. 1857.
Contains 104, 108.

78. *German Ballads and Poems,* with English Translations.
A. Boyd. Lond. Houston, 1857. 12.

79. *Goethe's Poems and Ballads.* Arthur Hugh Clough.
Critical article upon the translations of Aytoun and
Martin, with original translations. *Fraser's Mag.*
1859, LIX: 710; *Eclectic Mag.* Bost. 1860, XLV: 531.

Contains 6, 46, 66, 71, 72, 73, 166, 175, 198, 203, 212, 214,
215, 218, 221.

80. *The Roman Martyr,* A Dramatic Poem. "Nominis Umbra." Lond. Williams & Norgate. 1859. pp.111.
Contains in the appendix 1, 193, 226, 371, 384.

81. *Life Without and Within.* Margaret Fuller Ossoli. Bost.
Brown, Taggert & Chase, 1859. pp. 424. 16; N. Y.
Sheldon; Phil. Lippincott; Lond. Sampson.
Contains 64, 70, 72, 172, 176, 368.

82. *Poems Translated from the German.* J. C. Mangan. N. Y.

Haverty. 1859. pp. 460. For contents see No. 47.

E.—Translations Of Individual Poems Prior To 1860 (vol. I) Lteder 1.
Zueignung (Der Morgen ham). 1824.
Dedication, N. 0. H. I. *L. Mag.* IX: 186.
1839. *Inscription,* Dwight. Poems. Bost.
1844. *Dedication,* Aytoun-Martin.
Blackwood's Mag. LVI:54. Edin. 1853.
Dedication, Bowring. Poems. Lond.
1855. *Dedication,* M. A. Burt. Specimens, etc. Lond. 1859. *Dedication,* Aytoun-Martin. Poems. Lond. N. Y. 1859.
Dedication, Nominis Umbra. Lond. 2.
Vorklage. 1839. *Apology,* Dwight.
Poems. Bost. 1855. *Apology,* M. A. Burt. Specimens, etc. Lond. 1859. *Deprecation,* Thomas. Poems. Phil. 3. *An die Giinstigen.* 1839. *To the Friendly,* Dwight. Poems. Bost. 1839. *To the Gentle Reader,* Robt. Fraser. *Poetical Remains.* Lond. 1853. *To the Kind Reader,* Bowring. Poems. Lond. 1855. *To the Benevolent,* M. A. Burt. Specimens etc. Lond.
1859. *To the Friendly,* Thomas. Poems. Phil.
"Titles of the poems and their order have been given as in the Weimar Edition of Goethe's works. Bowring, Dwight, Aytoun-Martin and Thomas, each has a large number of these poems to which repeated reference must be made; therefore simply the name and the word "Poems" is given in these lists. For fuller details refer to the preceding bibliographies, C and D, both of which

are chronologically arranged.

Many of these versions, particularly the early ones, were printed anonymously. In some cases I have been able later to identify the author. The name has then been placed in parenthesis to indicate this. As far as possible, I have tried to give the place of publication of the various books, magazines, and Journals, in order to show how widespread or how limited were the various translations. Practically all poems here given have been examined and compared, so that even when the titles are identical, the poems are not duplicates, unless it is so stated in the list.

4. *Der neue Amadis.* 1853. *The new Amadis,* Bowring. Poems. Lond.
1855. *The new Amadis,* M. A. Burt. Specimens etc. Lond.
1859. *The new Amadis,* Aytoun-Martin. Poems. Lond. N. Y.

5. *Stirbt der Fuchs.* 1853. *When the Fox Dies,* Bowring. Poems. Lond. 1855. *When the Fox Dies,* M. A. Burt. Specimens etc. Lond. 1859. *Jack's Alive,* Thomas. Poems. Phil. 6. *Heidenroslein,* 1822. *The Rosebud,* "T". (Colburn's) *New Mo. Mag.*
V: 309. N. Y., Bost., Lond. 1824. Same version, *Canadian Mag.* III: 211. Montreal. 1826. *Rose upon the Lea,* G. Bancroft. *Atkinson's Casket.* I: 392. Phil.
1826. Same version, *Literary Casket.* I:168. Hartford, Conn.
1827. Same version, *Atlantic Souvenir.* Bost. 1836. *The Rosebud,* J. J. Campbell. *Song of the Bell,* etc. Edin. 1836.
Heather Rose, (J. C. Mangan) *Dublin TJniv. Mag.* VII: 298. 1843. *Little Red Rose,* J. B. *Tait's Edin. Mag.* X: 420.
1844. *The Wild Rose,* (Th. Martin) *Blackwood's Mag.* LVI: 417. Lond., Edin. 1852. *Rosebud on the Heather,* Mrs. Haller. Transla tions. Lond., Hamburg. 1853. *Rosebud on the Heath,* A. Baskerville. *Poetry of Ger.* Lond., N. Y., Phil., Leip. 1853. *The Heath Rose,* Bowring. Poems. Lond. 1855. *The Wood Rose,* M. A. Burt. Specimens, etc. Lond.
1859. *The Wild Rose,* Aytoun-Martin.

Poems. Lond., N. Y. 1859. Same version, *Fraser's Mag.* LIX: 714. Lond. 1859. *The Wild Rose,* Thomas. Poems. Phil. 7. *Blinde Kuh.* 1853. *Blindman's Buff,* Bowring. Poems. Lond. 1855. *Blindman's Buff,* M. A. Burt. Specimens, etc. Lond.
1859. *Blindman's Buff,* Thomas. Poems. Phil. 8. *Christel.* 1853. *Christel,,* Bowring. Poems. Lond. 1855. *Christine,* M. A. Burt. Specimens, etc. Lond. 9. *Die Sprdde.* 1850. *Coy Shepherdess,* Anon. *Tait's Edin. Mag.,* XVII: 274.
1853. *The Prude,* A. Baskerville. *Poetry of Ger.* Lond.,
N. Y., Phil., Leip. 1853. *The Coy One,* Bowring. Poems. Lond. 1855. *The Prude,* M. A. Burt. Specimens, etc. Lond. 1859. *The Coquette,* Aytoun-Martin. Poems. Lond.,
N. y.
1859. *The Prude,* Thomas. Poems. Phil. 10. *Die Bekehrte.* 1850. *The Shepherdess Caught,* Tait's *Edin. Mag.* XVII: 274. 1853. *The Convert,* A. Baskerville. *Poetry of Ger.*
Lond., N. Y., Phil., Leip. 1853. *The Convert,* Bowring. Poems. Lond. 1855. *The Convert,* M. A. Burt. Specimens, etc. Lond. 1859. *Smitten,* Aytoun-Martin. Poems. Lond., N. Y. 1859. *The Convert,* Thomas. Phil.
11. *Rettung.* 1852. *The Rescue,* Mrs. Haller. Translations, etc. Lond., Hamburg.
1853. *Preservation,* Bowring. Poems. Lond. 1859. *Just in Time,* Aytoun-Martin. Poems. Lond., N. Y. 1859. *Rescue,* Thomas. Poems. Phil. 12. *Der Musensohn.* 1839. *The Son of the Muses,* Dwight. Poems. Bost.
1853. *The Muses' Son,* Bowring. Poems. Lond.
1855. *Son of the Muses,* M. A. Burt. Specimens, etc. Lond. 13. *Gefunden.* 1845. *Found,* J. Gostwick. *Spirit of German Poetry.* Lond. 1853. *Found,* A. Baskerville. *Poetry of Ger.* Lond.,
N. Y., Phil., Leip. 1853. *Found,* Bowring. Poems. Lond. 1855. *Flower of the Forest,* M. A. Burt. Specimens, etc. Lond.

1859. *Treasure Trove,* Aytoun-Martin. Lond., N. Y. 1860. *Found,* J. D. Strong. *Hesperian Mag.* III: 502. San Francisco.
14. *Gleich und Gleich.* 1839. *Like to Like,* Rob't Fraser. Poetical Remains. Lond. 1853. *Like to Like,* A. Baskerville. *Poetry of Germany.* Lond., N. Y., Phil., Leip. 1853. *Like and Like,* Bowring. Poems. Lond. 1855. *Sympathetic Companions,* M. A. Burt.' Specimens, etc. Lond. 15. *Wechsellied zum Tanze.* 1853. *Reciprocal Invitation to the Dance,* Bowring. Poems. Lond. 1855. *Alternate Songs for the Dance,* M. A. Burt. Specimens, etc. Lond. 16. *Selbtsbetrug.* 1833; *Self Deceit,* Anon. *Mo. Mag.* XVI: 35. Lond. 1839. *Self Deception,* Dwight. Poems. Bost. 1839. Same version, *Western Messenger.* VI: 259. Louisville, Cincinnati.
1853. *Self Deceit,* Bowring. Poems. Lond.
1855. *Self Deception,* 1L A. Burt. Specimens, etc. Lond. 1859. *Self Deception,* Thomas. Poems. Phil. 17. *Krugserkldrung.* 1853. *Declaration of War,* Bowring. Poems. Lond. 1855. *Declaration of War,* M. A. Burt. Specimens etc. Lend. 18. *Liebhaber in alien Gestalten.* 1853. *Lover in all Shapes,* Bow ring. Poems. Lond.
1855. *Lover under Many Forms,* M. A. Burt. Specimens, etc. Lond.
1859. *Multiform Lover,* Thomas. Poems. Phil.
19. *Der Goldschmiedsgesell.* 1853. *The Goldsmith's Apprentice,* Bo wring. Poems. Lond. 1855. *The Goldsmith's Companion,* M. A. Burt. Specimens, etc. Lond. 20. *Antworten bei einem geseUschaftlichen Fragespiel.* 1850. *Answers for a Company,* S. E. B. *Democratic Rtv.* XXII: 132. X. T. 1852. *Answers to Questions,* (Mrs. A. Haller) Translations etc. Lond., Hamburg. 1852. *Answers in a Game of Questions,* Bowring. Poems. Lond. 1855. *Anwsers on Conversation Cards,* M. A. Burt. Specimens etc. Lond.
21. *Verschiedene Empfindungen an einem Platze.* 1853. *Different Emotions on the same Spot,* Bowring. Poems. Lond.

22. *Wer kauft Liebesgottert* 1844. *WhoU buy a Cupidf* (Aytoun) *Blackwood's Mag.* LVI: 62. Edin. 1853. *Wholl buy Gods of Love?* Bowring. Poems. Lond.
1859. Same as 1844. Aytoun-Martin. Poems. Lond., N. Y. 23. *Der Abschied.* (Lass mein Aug' den Abschied sagen) 1828. *0 Let Me Look Farewell,* Anon. *Lond. Weekly Rev.*
1828. Same version, *Museum of Foreign Lit.* XIII: 15. Phil.
1836. *Farewell,* J. J. Campbell. *Song of the Bell* etc. Bdin.
1839. *The Parting,* Dwight. Poems. Bost.
1839. *The Farewell,* Mrs. C. M. Sawyer. *New Yorker Mag.* VII: 195.
1840. Same as 1836, *Knickerbocker Mag.* XVI: 42. N. Y.
1841. Same as 1836, *Knickerbocker Mag.* XVII: 506. N. Y.
1842. *The Farewell,* Algernon. *Ideals.* Phil.
1850. *Parting,* C. E. Lambert. Poems. Lond.
1853. *The Farewell,* Bowring. Poems. Lond.
1859. *The Parting,* Aytoun-Martin. Poems. Lond., N. Y.
1859. Same version, *Littell's Living Age.* LXI: 185. Bost.
1859. *The Farewell,* Thomas. Poems. Phil.
24. *Die schbne Nacht.*
1830. *The Return,* Anon. *Literary Gem.* Lond.
1833. Same version, *Literary Rambler.* Edin.
1853. *The Beautiful Night.* Bowring. Poems.
1859. *Lovely Night,* Aytoun-Martin. Poems. Lond., N. Y.
1859. *Beautiful Night,* Thomas. Poems. Phil.
25. *Gliick und Traum.*

1849. *Love's Dream,* "Bon Gaultier", (Martin). *Dublin Univ. Mag.* XXXIII: 609.
1853. *Happiness and Vision,* Bowring. Poems. Lond.
1859. Same version as 1849, Aytoun-Martin. Poems. Lond., N. Y.
1859. *Joys and Dreams,* Thomas. Poems. Phil.
26. *Lebendiges Andenken.* 1853. *Living Bemembrance,* Bowring. Poems. Lond. 27. *Gliick der Entfernung.* 1839. *Joy of Separation,* Dwight. Poems. Bost. 1849. *The Bliss of Absence,* (Martin). *Dublin Univ. Mag.* XXXIII: 620. 1853. *The Bliss of Absence,* Bowring. Poems. Lond.
1859. Same as 1849, Aytoun-Martin. Poems. Lond., N. Y.
28. *An Luna.* 1853. *To Luna,* Bowring. Poems. Lond. 1859. *To Luna,* Aytoun-Martin. Poems. Lond., N. Y. 29. *Brautnacht.* 1853. *The Wedding Night,* Bowring. Poems. Lond. 30. *Schadenfreude.* 1844. *Second Life,* (Aytoun). *Blackwood's Mag.* LVI: 62. Edin. 1853. *Mischievous Joy,* Bowring. Poems. Lond.
1859. Same as 1844, Aytoun-Martin. Poems. Lond., N. Y.
31. *Unschuld.* 1839. *Innocence,* Dwight. Poems. Bost. 32. *Scheintod.* 1828. *Semblance of Death,* Rob't Robinson. Specimens, etc. Lond. 1845. *Death Trance,* (Martin). *Blackwood's Mag.* LVII: 177. Edin.
1853. *Apparent Death,* Bowring. Poems. Lond.
1859. *Love's Grave,* Thomas. Poems. Phil.
33. *Novemberlied.* 1839. *November Song,* Dwight. Poems. Bost.
1853. *November Song,* Bowring. Poems. Lond.
1859. *November Song,* Thomas. Poems. Phil.
34. *An die Erwahlte.*
1827. *To the Chosen One,* Chas. Des Voeux. *Tasso,* etc. Lond.
1853. *To the Chosen One,* Bowring. Poems. Lond.
1859. *To the Betrothed,* Aytoun-Martin.

Poems. Lond.,
N. Y.
1859. *To the Chosen,* Thomas. Poems.
Phil.
35. *Erster Verlust.*
1833. *First Love,* Anon. *Mo. Mag.* XVI:
35. Lond.
1844. *First Love,* (Martin). *Blackwood's Mag.* LVI:
61. Edin.
1853. *First Loss,* Bowring. Poems.
Lond.
1859. Same as 1844, Aytoun-Martin.
Poems. Lond.,
N. Y.
36. *Nachgefilhl.*
1853. *After Sensations,* Bowring.
Poems. Lond.
1859. *Sympathy,* Thomas. Poems. Phil.
37. *Nahe des Geliebten.*
1820. *I think of thee,* (Beresford) *Lays of a Wanderer.*
Lond.
1827. *Proximity to the Beloved One,* C.
Des Voeux.
Tasso etc. Lond.
1828. *I think of thee,* F. Page. Employment. Bath.
Eng.
1828. *I think of thee,* Robt. Eobinson.
Specimens etc.
Lond.
1828. *I think of thee,* Anon. *Weekly Rev.*
Lond.
1828. Same as preceding, *Museum of For. Lit.* XIII:45.
Phil.
1830. Same as preceding, "Y". *Fraser's Mag.* I:554.
  Lond.
1831. *Loved One Ever Near,* Anon.
Edin. Lit. Jour.
  V: 185.
1833. *Loved One Ever Near,* Anon. *Mo. Mag.* XVI: 35.
Lond.
1835. *I think of thee,* L. E. L(andon).
Lit. Gazette.
p. 11. Lond.
1836. *Nearness of the Beloved,* J. J.
Campbell. *Song of the Bell, etc.* Edin.
1839. *Loved One Ever Near,* Dwight,
Poems. Bost. 1839. *Forever Thine,* W.
F. (an imitation) *New Yorker Mag.* VIII:
180. 1839. *Presence of the Beloved,*

Mrs. C. M. Sawyer.
New Yorker VIII: 180. 1843. *I think of thee,* J. S. B. *Tait's Edin. Mag.*
X: 483.
1844. *7 think of thee,* Wm. C. Bryant.
Godey's Lady's Book. XXVIII: 41. Phil.
1844. *To Laura,* L. F. Klipstein. Orion,
Georgia. IV: 75. 1844. *I think of thee,* J.
H. Merivale. Poems. Lond. 1844. *Sepa-
ration,* (Aytoun) *Blackwood's Mag.* LVI:
430. Edin. 1845. Same as 1839, Dwight,
in Lonfellow's *Poets of Europe.* Lond.,
Phil. 1850. *Loved One Ever Near,* C. R.
Lambert. Poems etc.
Lond.
1851. *7 think of thee,* Anon. *Fraser's Mag.* XLIII: 113.
Lond.
1851. Same version, *Eclectic Mag.*
XXII: 539. N. Y. 1853. *Proximity of the Beloved,* Bowring. Poems. Lond. 1859.
Same as 1844, Aytoun-Martin. Poems.
Lond., N. Y. 1859. *Nearness of the Beloved,* Thomas. Poems. Phil. 38. *Ge-
genwart.* 1844. *To My Mistress,*
(Martin) *Blackwood's Mag.* LVI: 427.
Edin. 1853. *Presence,* Bowring. Poems.
Lond. 1859. Same version as 1844, Ay-
toun-Martin. Poems.
Lond., N. Y.
39. *An die Entfernte.* 1828. *To the Dis-
tant Fair,* Anon. *Weekly Rev.* Lond.
1828. Same version, *Museum of For.
Lit.* XIII: 16. Phil. 1828. *To One Re-
moved to a Distance,* R. Robinson.
Specimens etc. Lond. 1833. *Distant
One,* Anon. *L. Mo. Mag.* XVI: 35. Lond.
1842. *To the Parted One,* C. P. Cranch,
in *Brooks' Songs* etc. Bost., Lond. 1850.
Loved One Far Away, S. E. B. *Democratic Rev.* XXVII: 146. N. Y. 1853. *To the
Distant One,* Bowring. Poems. Lond.
1859. *In Absence,* Aytoun-Martin.
Poems. Lond., N. Y. 1859. *To the Dis-
tant,* Thomas. Poems. Phil.
40. *Am Flusse.* 1828. *By a River,* R.
Robinson. Specimens etc. Bost.
1853. *By the River,* Bowring. Poems.
Lond.
1859. *By the River,* Thomas. Poems.
Phil.
41. *Die Freuden.* 1819. *Our Joys,* Anon.
Blackwood's Mag. IV: 404. Edin. 1824.
Joy, George Bancroft. *N. Amer. Rev.*
XIX: 306. Bost. 1824. Same version,

Bancroft, *Life and Genius of Goethe.*
Bost. 1836. Same version as 1819, in
Bokum's *Ger. Wreath.*
Bost.
1839. Same version as 1824, in
Dwight's Poems. Bost.
1850. *Joy,* C. R. Lambert. Poems, etc.
Lond.
1853. *Joy,* Bowring. Poems. Lond.
1859. Same as 1850, *Russell's Mag.* VI:
108. Charleston, S. C.
1859. *Joy,* Thomas. Poems. Phil.
42. *Abschied.* (Zu lieblich ist's, ein
Wort zu brechen) 1853. *Farewell,*
Bowring. Poems. Lond. 43. *Wechsel.*
1853. *The Exchange,* Bowring. Poems.
Lond.
1859. *Change,* Thomas. Poems. Phil.
44. *Beherzigung.* 1839. *Musings,*
Dwight. Poems. Bost. 1844. *Encouragement,* J. H. Merivale. Poems. Lond.
1853. *The Rule of Life,* Bowring.
Poems. 45. *Meeres Stille.* 1845. *Calm
at Sea,* (Martin) *Blackwood's Mag.* LVII:
175. Edin. 1845. *Calm at Sea, "
Horus",* *Amer. Whig Mag.* I: 289. N. Y.
1848. *The Calm,* G. P. Maurer. *Collec-
tion of Poetry.* N. Y. 1853. *The Ocean
at Rest,* A. Baskerville. *Poetry of Ger.*
Lond., N. Y., Phil., Leip. 1853. *Calm
at Sea,* Bowring. Poems. Lond. 1859.
Calm at Sea, Aytoun-Martin. Poems.
Lond.,
  N. Y.
1859. *Calm at Sea,* Thomas. Poems.
Phil. 46. *GliickUche Fahrt.* 1845. *The
Breeze,* (Martin) *Blackwood's Mag.*
LVII: 173. Edin. 1848. *The Happy Voy-
age,* G. P. Maurer. *Collection of Poetry.*
N. Y. 1853. *The Prosperous Voyage,* A.
Baskerville. *Poetry of Ger.* Lond., N.
Y., Phil., Leip. 1853. *The Prosperous
Voyage,* Bowring. Poems. Lond. 1859.
Same as 1845, Aytoun-Martin. Poems.
Lond.,
N. Y.
1859. *The Prosperous Voyage,* Anon.
Fraser's Mag. LIX: 712. Lond. 47. *Mut.*
1853. *Courage,* Bowring. Poems. Lond.
48. *Erinnerung.* 1839. *Hint,* Dwight.
Poems. Bost.
1839. Same version, *Western Mess.* VII:
248. Louisville, Ky.
1848. *Admonition,* "H"(uddleston).
HaUeybury Ob-

server. V: 32. Conn.

1853. *Admonition,* Bowring. Poems. Lond.

1859. *Admonition,* Thomas. Poems. Phil.

49. *Willkommen und Abschied.*

1827. *Welcome and Farewell,* C. Des Voeux. *Tasso*
etc. Lond.

1841. Same version, *Democratic Rev.* IX: 589. N. Y.

1842. *Welcome and Farewell,* (E. Quinet). *Dem. Rev.*
X: 581. N. Y.

1845. *Welcome and Departure,* (Martin) *Blackwood's*
Mag. LVII: 472. Edin.

1853. *Welcome and Parting,* A. Baskerville. *Poetry of*
Ger. Lond., N. Y., Phil., Leip.

1853. *Welcome and Farewell,* Bowring. Poems. Lond.

1859. *Welcome and Farewell,* Thomas. Poems. Phil.

1859. Same as 1845, Aytoun-Martin. Poems. Lond.,
N. Y.

50. *Neue Liebe, neues Leben.*

1836. *New Love, New Life,* J. J. Campbell. *Song of*
the Bell etc. Lond.

1839. *New Love, New Life,* Dwight. Poems. Bost.

1839. *New Love, New Life,* Dwight. *N. Y. Rev.* IV: 393.

1839. *New Love, New Life,* Anon. *N. Y. Rev.* IV: 397.

1844. *New Love, New Life,* Anon. *Blackwood's Mag.*
LVI: 429. Edin.

1849. *New Love, New Life,* J. Oxenford. *Goethe's*
Autobiog. Lond.

1853. *New Love, New Life,* A. Baskerville, *Poetry of*
Germany. Lond., N. Y., Phil., Leip.

1853. *New Love, New Life,* Bowring. Poems. Lond.

1855. *New Love, New Life,* G. H. Lewes. *Life of*
Goethe. Lond., Bost.

1855. Same as 1849, Parke Godwin in *Goethe's Truth*
and Poetry. Bost., N. Y.

1859. *New Love, New Life,* Thomas.

Poems. Phil.

51. *An Belinden.* 1839. *To Belinda,* Dwight. Poems. Bost.

1848. *To Belinda,* J. Oxenford. *Goethe's Auto biography.* Lond. 1849. *To his Mistress,* "Bon Gaultier," (Martin) *Dub. Univ. Mag.* XXXIII: 608. 1853. *To Belinda,* Bowring. Poems. Lond. 1855. *To Belinda,* G. H. Lewes. *Life of Goethe.* Lond., Bost.

1855. Same as 1839, in Parke Godwin's *Truth and Poetry.* N. Y., Bost. 1859. Same as 1849, Aytoun-Martin. Poems. Lond., N. y.

1859. Same as 1848, *Littell's Liv. Age.* LXI: 184. Bost.

1859. Same as 1849, *Littell's Liv. Age.* LXI:184. Bost.

1859. *To Belinda,* prose version, Anon. *Littell's Liv. Age.* LXI: 184. Bost.

1859. *To Belinda,* Thomas. Poems. Phil.

52. *Mailied.* (Wie herrlich leuchtet) 1849. *May Song,* "Bon Gaultier", (Martin). *Dub. Univ. Mag.* XXXIII: 609. 1853. *May Song,* A. Baskerville, *Poetry of Ger.* Lond., N. Y. Phil, Leip.

1853. *May Song,* Bowring. Poems. Lond.

1856. *May Song,* Anon. *Blackwood's Mag.* LXXX: 422. Edin.

1859. Same as 1849, Aytoun-Martin. Poems. Lond., N. Y. 1859. *May Song,* Thomas. Poems. Phil. 1860. *May Song,* J. Benton. *The Dial.* I: 477. Cinn. 53. *Mit einem gemalten Bande.* 1849. *With an Embroidered Ribbon,* "Bon Gaultier", (Martin). *Dub. Univ. Mag.* XXXIII: 608. 1853. *With a Painted Ribbon,* Bowring. Poems. Lond. 1859. Same as 1849, Aytoun-Martin. Poems. Lond.. N. Y. 1859. *With a Painted Ribbon,* Thomas. Poems. Phil. 54. *Mit einem goldnen Halskettchen.*

1853. *With a Gold Necklace,* Bowring. Poems. Lond.

1859. *With a Gold Necklace,* Aytoun-Martin. Poems. Lond., N. Y.

1859. *With a Gold Chain,* Thomas. Poems. Phil.

55. *An Lottchen.*

1853. *To Charlotte,* Bowring. Poems. Lond.

56. *Auf dem See.*

1839. *On the Lake,* Dwight. Poems. Bost.

1849. *On the Lake,* J. Oxenford. *Goethe's Autobiog.* Lond.

1853. *On the Lake,* Bowring. Poems. Lond.

1856. *On the Lake,* Anon. *Littell's Living Age.* L: 18. Bost.

1859. *On the Lake,* Aytoun-Martin. Poems. Lond., N. y.

1859. *On the Lake,* Thomas. Poems. Phil.

57. *Vom Berge.*

1839. *From the Mountain,* Dwight. Poems. Bost.

1849. *To Lili,* J. Oxenford. *Goethe's Autobiog.* Lond.

1853. *From the Mountain,* Bowring. Poems. Lond.

1855. *From the Mountain,* G. H. Lewes. *Life of Goethe.* Lond., Bost.

1859. *From the Mountain,* Aytoun-Martin. Poems. Lond., N. Y.

1859. *From the Mountain,* Thomas. Poems. Phil.

58. *Blumengruss.*

1853. *Flower Salute,* Bowring. Poems. Lond.

59. *Mailied.* (Zwischen Weizen und Korn.)

1839. *May Song,* Dwight. Poems. Bost.

1839. Same version, *N. Amer. Rev.* XLVIII: 510. Bost.

1853. *May Song,* Bowring. Poems. Lond.

1859. *May Song,* Thomas. Poems. Phil. 60. *Fruhzeitiger Fruhling.* 1853. *Early Spring,* A. Baskerville. *Poetry of Germany.* Lond., N. Y., Phil., Leip. 1853. *Premature Spring,* Bowring. Poems. Lond. 1856. *Early Spring,* Anon. *Blackwood's Mag.* LXXX: 423. Bdin.

1859. *Early Spring,* Aytoun-Martin. Poems. Lond., N. Y. 61. *Herbstgefiihl.* 1853. *Autumn Feelings,* Bowring. Poems. Lond. 62. *Rastlose Liebe.* 1839.

Restless Love, Dwight. Poems. Bost. 1853. *Restless Love,* Bowring. Poems. Lond.

1856. *Restless Love,* Anon. *Black-wood's Mag.* LXXX: 410. Edin.

63. *Schafers Klagelied.* 1827. *Shepherd's Lament,* C. Des Voeux. *Tasso* etc. Lond.

1828. *Shepherd's Lament,* Anon. Lond. *Weekly Rev.* 1828. Same version, Anon. *Museum of For. Lit.* XIII: 15. Phil. 1831. Same version, *Fraser's Mag.* II: 232. Lond. 1852. *Shepherd's Complaint,* Mrs. A. Haller. Trans lations etc. Lond., Hamburg. 1853. *Shepherd's Lament,* A. Baskerville. *Poetry of Germany.* Lond. , N. Y., Phil., Leip. 1853. *Shepherd's Lament,* Bowring. Poems. Lond. 1859. *Shepherd's Lament,* Aytoun-Martin. Poems. Lond., N. Y.

1859. *Shepherd's Lament,* Thomas. Poems. Phil. 64. *Trost in Tranen.* 1827. *Consolation in Tears,* C. Des Voeux. *Tasso* etc. Lond. 1836. *Consolation in Tears,* J. J. Campbell, *Song of the Bell* etc. Lond. 1839. *Solace,* Dwight. Poems. Bost.

1845. Same version, in Longfellow's *Poets of Europe.* Lond., Phil.

1852. *Comfort in Tears,* Mrs. A. Haller. Translations etc. Lond., Hamburg.

1853. *Consolation in Tears,* A. Baskerville. *Poetry of Germany.* Lond., N. Y., Phil., Leip.

1853. *Comfort in Tears,* Bowring. Poems. Lond.

1856. *Comfort in Tears,* W. B. Rands, *Tait's Edin. Mag.* XXIII: 215.

1859. *Comfort in Tears,* Aytoun-Martin. Poems. Lond., N. Y.

1859. *The Consolers,* Marg. Fuller Ossoli. *Life With-out and Within.* Bost., N. Y., Phil. 65. *Nachtgesang.*

1830. *Serenade,* Anon. *Literary Gem.* Lond.

1833. *Serenade,* Anon. *Literary Rambler.* Edin.

1837. *Serenade,* "Y". *Tait's Edin. Mag.*

IV: 23.

1853. *Night Song.* Bowring. Poems. Lond.

66. *Sehnsucht.* (Was zieht mir das Herz so.)

1839. *Longings,* Dwight. Poems. Bost.

1853. *Longings,* Bowring. Poems. Lond.

1859. *Longings,* Aytoun-Martin. Poems. Lond.,N. Y.

1859. *Longings,* Same version, *Fraser's Mag.* LIX: 714. Lond.

67. *An Mignon.*

1853. *To Mignon,* Bowring. Poems. Lond.

68. *Bergschloss.*

1844. *Castle on the Mountain,* (Martin) *L. Mirror.* XLIV:375. (Wrongly attributed to Bulwer Lytton.)

1844. Same verison, (Martin) *Black-wood's Mag.* LVI: 425. Edin.

1845. *Castle on the Hill,* J. Gostwick. *Spirit of Ger. Poetry.* Lond.

1853. *The Mountain Castle,* Bowring. Poems. Lond.

1856. *Hill Castle.* Anon. *National Rev.* Lond.

1856. Same version, Anon. *Littell's Liv. Age.* L: 28. Bost.

1859. Same as 1844, Aytoun-Martin. Poems. Lond., N. Y.

1859. *Ruined Castle,* Thomas. Poems. Phil.

69. *Geistesgruss.* 1806. *Spirit's Greeting,* Anon. *L. Mo. Repository.* I:56.

1824. *Salutation of a Spirit,* G. Bancroft. *N. Amer. Rev.* XIX: 306. Bost. 1824. Same version, G. Bancroft. *Life and Genius of Goethe.* Bost. 1824. Same version, *L. Mo. Mag.* LVIII: 144. 1830. *The Sea-Mark,* Wm. Taylor. *Hist. Survey of Ger. Poetry.* Lond. 1836. *Voice from the Invisible World,* (J. C. Mangan) *Dub. Univ. Mag.* VII: 299. 1839. Same as 1824, in Dwight's Poems. Bost. 1845. Same as 1824, in Longfellow's *Poets of Europe.* Lond., Phil.

1845. Same as 1836, Mangan's *Ger. Anthology.* Dub. 1850. *Spirit Greeting,* F. H. Hedge, in *Furness' Song of the Bell,* etc. Phil. 1852. *Spirit Greeting,* Mrs. A. Haller. Translations etc. Lond. 1853. *Spirit's Salute,* Bowring. Poems. Lond. 1853. *Spirit's Greeting,* F. H. Hedge, *Gems of Ger. Verse.* Phil, N. Y. 1859. *Spirit's Greeting,* Aytoun-Martin. Poems. Lond., N. Y.

1859. *Spirit's Greeting,* Thomas. Poems. Phil. 70. *An ein goldnes Herz.*

1839. *To a Golden Heart,* Marg. Fuller, in Dwight's Poems. Bost. 1845. *To a Golden Heart,* (Aytoun) *Blackwood's Mag.* LVII: 171. Edin. 1847. *To a Golden Heart,* F. H. Hedge. *Prose Writers of Ger.* p. 263. Bost.

1849. *To a Golden Heart,* J. Oxenford. *Goethe's Auto-biog.* Lond.

1852. *To a Golden Heart,* (Mrs. A. Haller). Translations etc. Lond., Hamburg.

1853. *To a Golden Heart,* Bowring. Poems. Lond.

1855. Same as 1839, in Godwin's *Truth and Poetry.* Bost., N. Y.

1859. Same as 1845, Aytoun-Martin. Poems. Lond., N. Y.

1859. Same as 1839, *Life Within and Without.* Bost.

1859. *To a Golden Heart,* Thomas. Poems. Phil.

71. *Wonne der Wehmut.*

1800. *Bliss of Sorrow,* Anon. *L. Mo. Mag.* X: 46.

1801. Same version, Anon. *Poetical Register.* I: 210. Lond.

1841. *Strength of Sorrow,* Lord Lindsay. Ballads etc. Lond.

1845. *Sorrow without Consolation,* (Aytoun) *Black-wood's Mag.* LVII: 170. Edin.

1852. *Charm of Sadness,* Mrs. A. Haller. Translations etc. Lond., Hamburg.

1853. *Bliss of Sorrow,* Bowring. Poems. Lond.

1859. Same as 1845, *Fraser's Mag.* LIX:

714. Lond.
1859. Same as 1845, Aytoun-Martin. Poems. Lond.,
  N. Y.
72. *Wandrers Nachtlied.* (Der du von dem Himmel bist.)
1827. *Wanderer's Night Lay,* C. Des Voeux. *Tasso*
etc. Lond.
1828. *Wanderer's Night Song,* Anon. *L. Weekly Rev.*
1828. Same version, *Museum of For. Lit.* XIII: 16.
  Phil.
1837. *Wanderer's Night Song,* B. von Arnim. *Goethe's*
Correspondence with a Child. Lond.
1840. *Wanderer's Night Song,* B. von Arnim. *Goethe's*
Correspondence with a Child. Bost.
1845. *Wanderer's Night Song,* H. W. Longfellow.
Poets of Europe. Lond., Phil. 1845. *Wanderer's Night Song,* (Martin) *Blackwood's Mag.* LVII: 173. Edin. 1852. *Wanderer's Night Song,* Mrs. A. Haller. *Trans lations* etc. Lond., Hamburg. 1853. *Wanderer's Night Song,* Bowring. Poems. Lond. 1859. *Wanderer's Night Song,* A. H. Clough. *Fraser's Mag.* LIX: 710. Lond. 1859. *Wanderer's Night Song,* Thomas. Poems. Phil. 1859. Same as 1845, Aytoun-Martin. Poems. Lond.,
N. Y.
1859. Same as 1837, American Edition. Bost. 73. *Ein gleiches* (Ueber alien Gipfeln) 1833. *Night Song,* Mrs. Sarah Austin. *Goethe's Characteristics.* II: 161. Lond. 1844. *Night Song,* (Martin.) *Blackwood's Mag.* LVI: 546. Edin. 1845. *Night Song,* H. W. Longfellow. *Poets of Europe.*
Lond., Phil.
1852. *Night Song,* Mrs. A. Haller. *Translations* etc.
Lond., Hamburg.
1853. *Night Song,* Bowring. Poems. Lond. 1859. *Evening,* Aytoun-Martin. Poems. Lond., N. Y. 1859. *Night Song,* A. H. Clough. *Fraser's Mag.* LIX: 712. Lond. 1859. *Night Song,* H. W. Longfellow. *Fraser's Mag.* LIX: 712. Lond. (Not the same version as in 1845.
) 74. *Jagers Abendlied.* 1822. *Hunter's*

Evening Lay, (Beresford.) Specimens etc. Lond. 1828. *Hunter's Evening Lay,* R. Robinson. Specimens etc. Lond. 1852. *Hunter's Evening Song,* Mrs. A. Haller. Trans lations etc. Lond., Hamburg. 1853. *Hunter's Even Song,* Bowring. Poems. Lond. 1859. *Huntsman's Evening Song,* Aytoun-Martin. Poems. Lond., N. Y.
1859. *Huntsman's Evening Song,* Thomas. Poems. Phil.
75. *An den Mond.*
1798. *Moonlight,* (Beresford.) *German Erato.* Berlin,
Lond.
1798. *Moonlight,* (Beresford.) *German Songster.* Berlin, Lond.
1800. *Moonlight,* (Beresford.) *Ladies' Mag.* LXXXI: 158. Lond.
1821. *Moonlight,* (Beresford.) *Specimens of Ger. Lyric Poets.* Lond.
1827. *To the Moon,* C. Des Voeux. *Tasso* etc. Lond.
1828. *To the Moon, Weekly Rev.* Lond.
1828. Same version, *Museum of For. Lit.* XIII: 16.
Phil.
1836. Same version as 1798, in *Bokum's Ger. Wreath.*
Bost.
1839. *To the Moon.* Dwight. Poems. Bost.
1845. Same version, in Longfellow's *Poets of Europe.*
Lond., Phil.
1852. *To the Moon,* Mrs. A. Haller. Translations etc.
  Lond., Hamburg.
1853. *To the Moon,* A. Baskerville. *Poetry of Germany.*
Lond., N. Y., Phil., Leip.
1853. *To the Moon,* Bowring. Poems. Lond.
1859. *To the Moon,* Aytoun-Martin. Poems. Lond.,
  N. Y.
1859. *To the Moon,* Thomas. Poems. Phil.
76. *Einschrankung.*
1839. *Confinement,* Dwight. Poems. Bost
77. *Hoffnung.*

1839. *Hope,* Dwight. Poems. Bost.
78. *Sorge.*
1839. *Care,* Dwight. Poems. Bost.
79. *Eigentum.* 1839. *Property,* Dwight. Poems. Bost.
1853. *My only Property.* Bowring. Poems. Lond. 80. *An Lina.* 1839. *To Lina,* Dwight. Poems. Bost.
1839. *To Lina,* Dwight, *Western Messenger.* VI: 359.
Louisville.
1853. *To Lina,* Bowring. Poems. Lond.
1859. *To Lina,* Aytoun-Martin. Poems. Lond., N. Y. 1859. *To Lina,* Thomas. Poems. Phil. GESELLIGE LIEDER 81. *Zum neuen Jahr.* 1853. *On ike New Year,* Bowring. Poems. Lond. 82. *Stiftungslied.* 1853. *Anniversary Song,* Bowring. Poems. Lond. 83. *Friihlingsorakel.* 1839. *Spring Oracle,* Dwight. Poems. Bost.
1853. *Oracle of Spring,* A. Baskerville. *Poetry of Germany.* Lond., N. Y., Phil., Leip.
1853. *The Spring Oracle,* Bowring. Poems. Lond.
1859. *The Spring Oracle,* Thomas. Poems. Phil.
84. *Die gliicklichen Gotten.* 1839. *For Life,* J. F. Clark, in Dwight's Poems. Bost. 1847. *The Happy Pair,* (Anon.) *Amer. Whig. Rev.*
V:122. N. Y. 1853. *The Happy Couple,* Bowring. Poems. Lond. 1859. *The Happy Couple,* Thomas. Poems. Phil. 1859. *The Happy Pair,* Aytoun-Martin. Poems. Lond.
  N. Y.
1859. Same version, *Littell's Living Age.* LXI: 185. Bost. 1859. Same version, *Harper's Mo. Mag.* XVIII: 705. N. Y. 85. *Bundeslied.*
1836. *Drinking Song.* J. J. Campbell. *Song of the Bell,* etc. Lond.
1839. *Song of Union,* Dwight. Poems. Bost.
1846. *Convivial Song,* Anon. *Tait's Edin.Mag.* XIII: 98.
1853. *Song of Fellowship,* Bowring. Poems. Lond.
86. *Dauer im Wechsel.*
1839. *Stability in Change,* N. L. Frothingham, in
Dwight's Poems. Bost.

1839. *Stability in Change,* S. Marg. Fuller, Bost. (Not published.).
1853. *Constancy in Change,* Bowring. Poems. Lond.
1855. Same as 1839, N. L. Frothingham. Metrical Pieces, etc. Bost.
87. *Tischlied.*
1832. *Table Song,* John Payne Collier. (Cited in *Goethe-Jahrbuch,* XXX: 220, 1909.)
1853. *Table Song,* Bowring. Poems. Lond.
88. *Gewohnt, getan.*
1836. *Wont and Done,* J. J. Campbell, *Song of the Bell,* etc. Lond.
1853. *Wont and Done,* Bowring. Poems. Lond.
89. *Generalbeichte.*
1839. *General Confession,* Dwight. Poems. Bost.
1839. *General Confession,* S. Naylor. A Drama, etc. Maidenhead, Eng.
1846. *General Confession,* Anon. *Tait's Edin. Mag.* XIII: 98.
1853. *General Confession,* Bowring. Poems. Lond.
90. Left unassigned through an error discovered too late for correction.
"Braun, F. A., *Margaret Fuller and Goethe,* pp. 216-241. Holt & Co., N. T., 1910.
91. *Kophtisches Lied.* 1836. *Song from the Coptic,* (J. C. Mangan.) *Dub. Univ. Mag.* VII: 293. 1839. *Cophtic Song,* Dwight. Poems. Bost. 1845. Same as 1836, Mangan's *Ger. Anthology.* Dublin. 1853. *Coptic Song,* Bowring. Poems. Lond. 1859. *Coptic Song,* Aytoun-Martin. Poems. Lond., N. Y.
1859. *Coptic Song,* Thomas. Poems. Phil. 92. *Ein anderes.* (Geh, gehorche meinen Winken) 1831. *World's Philosophy,* Anon. *Edin. Lit. Journal.* V:185.
1836. *A Second,* (J. C. Mangan) *Dub. Univ. Mag.* VII: 293. 1844. *Koptic Song.* J. H. Merivale. Specimens, etc. Lond.
1845. Same as 1836, Mangan's *Ger. An-*

thology. Dublin. 1853. *Another,* Bowring. Poems. Lond. 1859. *Another,* Thomas. Poems. Phil. 93. *Vanitas, vanitatum vanitas!* 1833. *Vanitas,* Mrs. Sarah Austin. *Goethe's Characteristics,* I:225. Lond. 1833. *Vanitas,* J. M. *Gentlemen's Mag.* CIII, part II, p. 138. Lond. 1836. *Vanitas,* L. J. B (ernays). *L. Mirror.* XXVII: 292. 1836. *Cosmopolite,* (J. C. Mangan) *Dub. Univ. Mag.* VII: 300. 1837. *Vanitas,* (J. S. Dwight) *Amer. Mo. Mag.* X: 361. N. y.
1838. *Vanitas,* M. N. *Tait's Edin. Mag.* V: 704. 1839. Same as 1837. Dwight. Poems. Bost. 1839. Same as 1837. Dwight. *Western Messenger.* VI: 259. Louisville. 1839. Same as 1837. Dwight. *N.Y.Bev.* IV: 393. 1839. *Vanitas,* Robt. Fraser. *Poetical Remains.* Lond.
1845. Same as 1837, Longfellow's *Poets of Europe.* Lond., Phil.
1853. *Vanitas,* Bowring. Poems. Lond.
1856. *Vanitas,* Anon. *Blackwood's Mag.* LXXX:413. Edin.
1859. *Vanitas,* Thomas. Poems. Phil.
94. *Kriegsgluck.*
1853. *Fortunes of War,* Bowring. Poems. Lond.
95. *Offene Tafel.*
1833. *Open Table,* Mrs. Sarah Austin. *Goethe's Characteristics.* IV: 344. Lond.
1839. *Open Table,* Dwight. Poems. Bost.
1853. *Open Table,* Bowring. Poems. Lond.
1859. *Open House,* Thomas. Poems. Phil.
96. *Rechenschaft.*
1839. *The Reckoning,* Dwight. Poems. Bost.
1853. *The Reckoning,* Bowring. Poems. Lond.
97. *Ergo bibamus!*
1836. *Ergo Bibamus,* J. J. Campbell. *Song of the Bell,* etc. Lond.
1853. *Ergo Bibamus,* Bowring. Poems. Lond.
98. *Epiphaniasfest.*
1853. *Epiphanias.* Bowring. Poems. Lond.

99. *Sizilianisches Lied.*
1853. *Sicilian Song.* Bowring. Poems. Lond.
100. *Schweizerlied.*
1836. *Swiss Song,* Mrs. E. Robinson. *N. Amer. Rev.* XXXVI: 266. N. Y., Bost.
1853. *Swiss Song,* Bowring. Poems. Lond.
101. *Finnisches Lied.*
1853. *Finnish Song,* Bowring. Poems. Lond.
102. *Zigeunerlied.* 1799. *Gipsy's Song,* Rose Lawrence. Translation of *Gotz.* Liverpool. 1799. *Gipsy's Song,* "Walter Scott. Translation of *Gotz.* Liverpool.
1833. *Gipsy's Song,* J. M. *Gentlemen's Mag.* CIII, part 2, p. 139. Lond. 1836. *Gipsy's Song,* J. J. Campbell. *Song of the Bell,* etc. Lond. 1836. *Gipsy's Song.* Anon. *Dub. Univ. Mag.* VIII: 360.
1850. *Gipsy's Song,* New edition of Scott's *Gotz,* Bohn. Lond.
1853. *Gipsy's Song,* Bowring. Poems. Lond.
1856. *Gipsy's Song,* Anon. *Blackwood's Mag.* LXXX:426. Edin.
BALLADEN 103. *Mignon.* 1798. *Mignon,* (Beresford.) *German Erato.* Berlin, Lond. 1798. The same version, *German Songster,* Berlin, Lond. 1814. *Mignon,* C. Kedding. *Mo. Mag.* XXXVIII: 45. Lond. 1817. Same as 1798, *N. Amer. Rev.* IV: 201. Bost., N. Y. (It is stated that this is translated "by a celebrated English Bard," but it is Beresford's.) 1821. Same as 1798, Specimens, etc. Lond. 1822. Same as 1798, *Athenaeum.* XI: 144. Bost.
1822. Same as 1798, *European Mag.* p. 157. Lond.
1822. *Mignon,* Anon. *Scot's Mag.* VII: 414. Edin.
1824. *Mignon,* Thos. Carlyle. Translation of *Wtihelm Meister.* Edin., Lond.
1824. *Mignon,* (R. Robinson) *Annual Rev.* LXVI: 286. Lond.
1824. *Mignon,* Anon. *Lond. Mag.* IX: 285. 1824. *Mignon,* J. C. H(are?) *Lond. Mag.* IX: 527. 1824. *Mignon,* G. Ban-

croft. *N. Amer. Rev.* XIX: 316.
Bost., N. Y.
1824. *Mignon, G.* Bancroft. *Life and Genius of Goethe.*
Bost.
1824. *Mignon,* Anon. *Kaleidoscope.* IV: 432. Liverpool.
1825. *Mignon,* Anon. *Edin. Rev.* XLII: 428.
1825. Same as 1824, Robinson. *Cabinet of Poetry and Romance.* Lond.
1827. *Mignon,* C. Des Voeux. *Tasso,* etc. Lond.
1828. Same as 1824, Robinson. *Specimens,* etc. Lond.
1828. Same as 1824, Robinson. *Athenaeum.* I: 501.
Lond.
1830. Same as 1798, in W. Taylor's *Hist. Survey of Ger. Poetry.* Lond.
1833. *Mignon,* Felicia Hemans. *Dub. Univ. Mag.*
II: 203. (Same version found in the collected poems of Mrs. Hemans and in Bryant's *New Library of Poetry,* p. 789. 1870.)
1833. *Mignon,* H H. J. *Blackwood's Mag.* XXXIII: 90.
Edin.
1835. *Mignon,* (C. J. Mangan.) *Dub. Univ. Mag.* V: 405.
1836. *Mignon,* J. J. Campbell. *Song of the Bell,* etc.
Lond.
1836. *Song,* same as 1798, in Bokum's *Ger. Wreath.*
Bost.
1838. *Mignon,* A. B. C. *Court Mag.* II: 249. Lond.
1838. *Mignon,* W. M. H. (Colburn's) *New Mo. Mag.*
LIV:553. Lond.
1839. *Mignon,* L. J. Bernays, *Selected Translations with Faust.* Lond.
1839. *Mignon,* W. H. Channing in Dwight's Poems.
Bost.
1840. *Mignon,* J. E. Reade. *The Drama of Life.* Lond.
1840. *Mignon,* Mrs. C. M. Sawyer. *New Yorker,* IX: 162.

N. y.
1842. *Mignon,* C. T. Brooks. *Songs and Ballads.* Bost.,
Lond.
1844. *Mignon,* H. M. *Democratic Rev.* IV: 315. N. Y.' 1844. *Mignon,* (Aytoun-Martin.) *Blackwood's Mag.* LVI:64.
Edin.
1845. *Mignon,* (Aytoun-Martin.) *Christ. Parlor Mag.* II: 11. N. Y. (Wrongly attributed to Bulwer Lytton.)
1845. *Mignon,* same as 1835. Mangan's *Ger. Anthology.*
Dub.
1846. *Mignon,* J. Burns. *Ger. Ballads.* Lond. 1852. *Mignon,* Samuel T. Coleridge. *Poetic and Dramatic Works.* Lond. 1852. *Mignon,* Mrs. A. Haller. Translations, etc. Lond., Hamburg.
1853. *Mignon,* A. Baskerville. *Poetry of Germany.*
Lond., N. Y., Phil., Leip. 1853. *Mignon,* Bowring. Poems. Lond. 1855. *Mignon,* R. D. Boylan. Translation of *Wtthelm Meister.* Lond. 1855. *Mignon,* M. A. Burt. Specimens, etc. Lond. 1859. Same as 1844, Aytoun-Martin. Poems. Lond., N. Y.
1859. *Mignon, 3.* D. Strong. Hutching's *Cal. Mag.* III:323. San Fran.
1859. *Mignon,* Thomas. Poems. Phil.
104. *Der Sanger.* 1798. *The Harper's Song,* (Beresford) *German Erato.* Berlin, Lond. 1798. *The Minstrel,* same version, *German Songster.* Berlin, Lond.
1800. *The Minstrel,* same version, *Lady's Mag.* XXX: 220. Lond. 1800. *The Harper,* same version, *Collection of Ger. Ballads.* Berlin. 1820. *The Minstrel,* Anon. *Lays of a Wanderer.* Lond. 1821. Same as 1798, *Specimens of German Lyrics.* Lond. This same magazine contains a parody of *Mignon,* written as a religious poem. 1824. *The Singer,* Thomas Carlyle. *Wilhelm Meister.* Lond., Edin.
1825. *The Singer,* Thomas Carlyle. *L. Mo. Rev.* CVI: 529.
1828. *The Singer,* Thomas Carlyle. Amer. edition of *Wilhelm Meister.* Bost.
1829. *The Minstrel,* Anon. *Edin. Lit.*

Jour. I:290.
1833. Same as 1798, Wm. Taylor's *Hist. Survey of Ger. Poetry.* Lond.
1835. *The Minstrel,* (J. C. Mangan) *Dub. Univ. Mag.*
V:404.
1836. Same as 1798, Bokum's *Ger. Wreath.* Bost.
1839. *The Minstrel,* J. S. Dwight. Poems. Bost.
1841. *The Minstrel,* T. P. *Museum of For. Lit.* II:356.
Phil.
1844. *The Minstrel,* (Martin). *Blackwood's Mag.*
LVI:65. Edin.
1844. *The Minstrel,* M. M. A. *Dublin Citizen.* IV: 251.
1844. *The Minstrel,* L. F. Klipstein. *Orion.* IV: 161.
Georgia, U. S. A.
1845. Same as 1835, Mangan's *Ger. Anthology.* Dublin.
1845. *The Minstrel,* J. Burns. *Ger. Ballads.* Lond.
1850. *The Singer,* F. H. Hedge in Furness' *Song of the Bell* etc. Phil.
1852. *The Minstrel,* Mrs. A. H. Haller. Translations
etc. Lond.
1853. *The Minstrel,* A. Baskerville. *Poetry of Ger.*
Lond., N. Y., Phil., Leip.
1853. *The Minstrel,* Bowring. Poems. Lond.
1853. *The Minstrel,* R. D. Boylan. *Wilhelm Meister.*
Lond.
1853. Same as 1850, Furness' *Gems of Ger. Verse.* Phil.
1855. *The Minstrel,* M. A. Burt. Specimens etc. Lond.
1859. *The Minstrel,* Thomas. Poems. Phil.
1859. Same as 1844, Aytoun-Martin. Poems. Lond., N. Y.
105. *Das Veilchen.* 1798. *The Violet,* (Beresford) *German Erato.* Berlin, Lond.
1798. Same version, *German Songster.* Berlin, Lond. 1803. Same version, *L. Mo. Register.* II: 333. 1821. Same ver-

sion, *Specimens of Ger. Lyrics.* Lond. 1824. *The Violet,* George Bancroft. *N. Amer. Rev.* XIX: 317. Bost. 1827. *The Violet,* C. Des Voeux. *Tasso* etc. Lond. 1829. *The Violet,* Anon. *Edin. Lit. Jour.* I:290. 1833. Same as 1824, *Western Mo. Mag.* I:308. Cincinnati, 0. 1835. *The Violet* (J. C. Mangan) *Dub. Univ. Mag.* V:406.

1839. *The Violet,* Dwight. Poems. Bost. 1839. *The Primrose,* M. G. Lewes. *Life and Correspondence.* Lond.

1841. *The Violet,* M. M. A. *Dub. Citizen.* IV: 268. 1844. *The Violet,* (Martin) *Blackwood's Mag.* LVI: 66. Edin.

1845. *Acrostic from Goethe,* "M". *South. Lit. Mes senger.* XI: 118. Richmond, Va. 1845. Same as 1835, Mangan's *Ger. Anthology.* Dublin. 1852. *The Violet,* Mrs. A. Haller. Translations etc. Lond.

1853. *The Violet,* A. Baskerville. *Poetry of Ger.* Lond., N. Y., Phil., Leip. 1853. *The Violet,* Bowring. Poems. Lond. 1855. Same as 1824, Bancroft's *Essays and Misc.* Bost. 1859. Same as 1844, Aytoun-Martin. Poems. Lond., N. Y.

1859. *The Violet,* Thomas. Poems. Phil. 106. *Der untreue Kndbe.* 1801. *Frederick and Alice,* Walter Scott, in Lewis' *Tales of Wonder.* Lond. 1806. Same version, Scott's *Ballads and Lyrical Pieces.* Edin.

1807. Same version, *Portfolio,* new series, IV: 134. Phil. 1853. *The Faithless Boy,* Bowring. Poems. Lond. 1859. *The False Lover,* Aytoun-Martin. Poems. Lond., N. Y.

. *Der Erlkonig.*

1795. *The Erlking,* M. G. Lewis in *Ambrosio or the Monk.* Lond.

1796. Same version, *Mo. Mirror.* II: 371. Lond.

1797. *The Erlking,* Walter Scott. Privately printed. Edin.

1798. Same as 1795, *Weekly Mag.* III: 93. Phil.

1798. Same as 1795, Amer. edition of *The Monk.* Phil.

1798. *The King of the Deuses,* (Wm. Taylor). *Mo. Malg.* VI: 438. Lond.

1801. Same as 1797, Lewis' *Tales of Wonder.* Lond.

1806. Same as 1797, Scott's *Ballads and Lyrical Pieces.* Edin.

1808. Same as 1797, *Portfolio,* IV: 32. Phil.

1821. *The Erlking,* Anon. *Athenaeum.* X: 154. Bost.

1823. *The Erlking,* George 0. Borrow. *Mo. Mag.* LVI:438. Lond.

1824. Same version, *Athenaeum.* XIV: 439. Bost.

1827. *The Erlking,* C. Des Voeux. *Tasso* etc. Lond.

1830. *The Erlking,* D. H. L. *Athenaeum.* III:57. Lond.

1833. Same as 1798, Taylor's *Hist. Survey of Ger. Poetry.* Lond.

1833. *The Erlenkoenig,* E. Fehrmann. *Knickerbocker Mag.* II:197. N. Y.

1833. *The Wood Demon,* "L." *New Eng. Mag.* V:7. Bost.

1834. *The Erlking,* T. J. A. *Tait's Edin. Mag.* I:520.

1834. Same version, *Lond. Mirror.* XXIV: 421.

1835. *The Erlking,* H. Berkeley. *New Eng. Mag.* VIII: 371. Bost.

1836. *The Alder King,* (J. C. Mangan.) *Dub. Univ. Mag.* VII: 291.

1836. *The Erlking,* Anon. Library of Romance. Lond. 1836. Same as 1833, Fehrmann in Bokum's *Ger. Wreath.* Bost.

1839. *The Erlking,* F. H. Hedge in Dwight's Poems. Bost. 1839. *King of the Alders,* W. F. *New Yorker.* VIII: 210. 1841. *The Erlking,* Mary E. Lee. *Magnolia.* III: 131. Savannah. 1841. *The Erlking,* Lord Lindsay. *Ballads, etc.* Lond.

1842. *The Erlking,* C. T. Brooks. *Songs and Ballads.* Bost., Lond.

1843. *The Elfking,* L. F. Klipstein. *Magnolia.* New series, II: 374. Savannah.

1844. *The Erlking.* (Martin) *Blackwood's Mag.* LVI:63. Edin. 1845. Same as 1836, Mangan's *Ger. Anthology.* Dublin. 1848. *The Erlking,* G. P. Maurer, *Collection of Poetry.* N. Y.

1849. *The Erlking,* C. F. *Fraser's Mag.* XL: 276. Lond. 1850. Same as 1839, Hedge in Furness' *Song of the Bell.* Phil. 1852. *The Erlking,* L. J. L. *South Lit. Messenger.* XVIII: 352. Richmond., Va. 1853. *The Erlking,* A. Baskerville. *Poetry of Ger.* Lond., N. Y., Phil., Leip. 1853. Same as 1839, in Furness' *Gems of Ger. Verse.* Phil.

1853. *The Erlking,* Bowring Poems. Lond. 1855. *The Erlking,* M. A. Burt. Specimens, etc. Lond. 1855. *The Erlking,* A. C. Kendrick. Echoes etc. Rochester, N. Y., Chic. 1855. Same as 1839, Hedge in *Gleanings from the Poets.* Bost.

1859. *The Erlking,* Joel Benton. *Democratic Rev.* XL: 373. N. Y. This translation Is generally used with Schubert's music, Opus 21.

1859. Same as 1844, Aytoun-Martin. Poems. Lond., N. Y.

1859. *The Erlking,* J. Cochran. Hutching's *California Mag.* III: 505. San Fran.

1859. *The Erlking,* Mrs. J. A. Morgan. Privately circulated. Racine, Wis.

1859. *The Erlking,* Thomas. Poems. Phil.

The Erlking, J. G. Whittier, (Year of translation uncertain, but it probably is prior to 1860. See *Goethe-Jahrbuch,* XXV: 233, 1904. It is not included among his published poems.)

108. *Der Fischer.*

1798. *The Fisher,* (Beresford.) *German Erato.* Berlin, Lond.

1798. Same version, *German Songster.* Berlin, Lond.

1800. Same version, *Collection of Ger. Ballads.* Berlin.
1801. *The Fisherman,* M. G. Lewis. *The Monk.* Lond.
1817. *The Mermaid,* J. F. *Blackwood's Mag.* I:171.
Bdin.
1821. Same as 1798, *Specimens of Ger. Lyrics.* Lond.
1822. Same version, *European Mag.* p. 157. Lond.
1822. Same version, *Athenaeum,* p. 144. Bost.
1822. Same version, *Gentlemen's Mag.* II:415. Phil.
1822. *The Fisher,* Jane Welsh (Carlyle). Sent in a
letter to Thos. Carlyle.
1824. *The Angler,* George Bancroft. *N. Amer. Rev.*
XIX: 318. Bost.
1824. *The Fisher,* "G. M." *New Mo. Mag.* VII: 576.
    Lond.
1824. Same version, *New Mo. Mag.* VII: 576. Bost.
1829. *The Fisher,* Anon. *Edin. Lit. Jour.* I: 290.
1830. *The Mermaid.* Wm. Taylor. *Hist. Survey of Ger.*
Poetry. Lond.
1833. *The Fisher,* Anon. *Lit. Gazette.* XVII: 315.
    Lond.
1834. *The Fisher,* T. J. A. *Tait's Edin. Mag.* I: 804.
See *Love Letters of Jane Welsh and Thomas Carlyle,* edited by A
Carlyle. Published by Lane & Co., Lond., 1909.
1836. Same as 1817, in Bokum's *Ger. Wreath.* Bost.
1837. *The Fisher,* J. C. Mangan. *Dub. Univ. Mag.* IX: 284. 1838. *The Fisher,* Anon. *Gentleman's Mag.* II:415. Phil.
1839. *The Fisher,* Anon. *The Capuciner.* N. Y. 1839. *The Angler,* W. F. *New Yorker.* VIII: 210. 1839. *The Fisher,* Dwight. Poems. Bost. 1841. *The Fisher,* M. M. A. *Dub. Citizen.* IV: 228. 1841. *The Fisherman Caught,* Harriet Beecher Stowe. *Godey's Lady's Book.* XXIII: 11. Phil. 1841. *The Fisher,* Lord Lindsay. *Ballads.* Lond. 1842. *The Fisher,* C. T.

Brooks. *Songs and Ballads.* Bost., Lond.
1844. *The Fisher,* F. H. Hedge in *The Gift.* p. 182. Phil. 1844. *The Fisher,* (Martin.) *Blackwood's Mag.* LVI: 65. Edin. 1845. Same as 1837, Mangan's *Ger. Anthology.* Dublin. 1850. *The Fisher,* C. R. Lambert. Poems etc. Lond.
1852. *The Fisher,* Anon. *Dub. Univ. Mag.* XL: 581. 1852. *The Fisher,* Mrs. A. Haller. Translations etc. Lond.
1852. *The Fisher,* L. I. L. *South. Lit. Messenger.* XVIII: 352. Richmond, Va.
1853. *The Angler,* A. Baskerville. *Poetry of Ger.* Lond.,
N. Y., Phil., Leip. 1853. *The Fisher,* Bowring. Poems. Lond. 1853. *The Fisher,* Anon. *Thalatta.* Bost.
1855. *The Fisher,* G. H. Lewes. *Life of Goethe.* Lond.,
Bost.
1856. Same as 1842, in Bryant's *Anthology of Poetry.*
N. Y.
1857. Same as 1837, in *Household Book of Poetry.*
Edited by C. A. Dana. N. Y. 1859. Same as 1844, Aytoun-Martin. Poems. Lond.. N. Y.
1859. Same as 1844, *Littell's Living Age.* LXI:186. Bost. 1859. Same as 1844, *The Critic,* p. 824. Lond.
1859. *The Fisher,* Thomas. Poems. Phil. 109. *Der Kbnig in Thule.*
1821. *The King of Thule,* (Beresford.) *Specimens of*
Ger. Lyrics. Lond.
1823. *The King of Thule,* Francis Leveson Gower.
Translations etc. Lond.
1825. *The King of Thule,* Anon. *Lit. Gazette,* p. 796.
Lond.
1827. *The King in Thule,* C. Des Voeux. *Tasso* etc.
Lond.
1830. *The King of Thule,* Wm. Taylor. *Hist. Survey*
of Ger. Poetry. Lond.
1834. *The King in Thule,* T. J. A. *Tait's Edin. Mag.*
I:804.
1835. *The Monarch's Goblet,* G(rimke) D(ayton).

South. Lit. Jour. I:112. South Carolina.
1836. *The King of Thule,* J. J. Campbell. *Song of the*
Bell. Edin.
1836. Same as 1830, in Bokum's *Ger. Wreath.* Bost.
1837. *The King of Thule,* (J. C. Mangan.) *Dub. Univ.*
Mag. IX: 285.
1839. *The King of Thule,* Dwight. Poems. Bost.
1841. *The King of Thule,* M. M. A. *Dub. Citizen.*
IV: 268.
1841. *The King of Thule,* Lord Lindsay. *Ballads.* Lond.
1845. *The King of Thule,* (Aytoun-Martin) *Black-*
wood's Mag. LVII:166. Edin.
1845. *The King of Thule,* J. Gostwick. *Ger. Lit.* Lond.
1845. *The King of Thule,* J. Gostwick. *Spirit of Ger.*
Poetry. Lond. (Not the same version as the preceding.)
1845. Same as 1837, Mangan's *Ger. Anthology.* Dub.
1849. *The King of Thule,* C. F. *Fraser's Mag.* XL: 95.
    Lond.
1850. *The King of Thule,* C. R. Lambert. Poems etc.
    Lond.
TM Not Including the eighteen translations of *Faust,* part I.
1852. *The King of Thule,* Mrs. A. Haller. Translations etc. Lond.
1853. *The King of Thule,* Bowring. Poems. Lond.
1857. *The King of Thule,* G. Turner. *Train.* IV: 59.
Lond.
1859. *The King of Thule,* Aytoun-Martin. Poems.
Lond., N. Y. (Not the same as 1844.)
1859. *The King of Thule,* Martin. *Once A Week.*
    I:250. Lond. (Not the same as 1844.) 1859. *The King of Thule,* Thomas. Poems. Phil.
110. *Das Bliimlein Wunderschdn. (Lied des gefangnen Graf en.)* 1823. *Lay of the Imprisoned Knight,* Francis Leveson Gower. Translations. Lond.
1824. Same version, *Lit. Gazette,* p. 85.

Lond. 1824. *Song of the Captive Count,*
G. Bancroft. *N. Amer. Rev.* XIX: 319.
Bost. 1827. *Flowret Wondrous Fair,* C.
Des Voeux. *Tasso.*
Lond.
1835. *The Lovely Little Flower,* L. E.
L(andon). *Lit. Gazette,* p. 11. Lond.
1836. *Song of the Imprisoned Count,*
J. J. Campbell. *Song of the Bell.* Lond.
1836. *Lay of the Captive Count,* (J. C.
Mangan.) *Dub. Univ. Mag.* VII: 290.
1839. *The Wonderful Flower,* Anon. *The
Capuciner.*
N. Y.
1839. *The Flowret Wondrous Fair,*
Dwight, Poems.
Bost.
1841. *The Imprisoned Knight,* M. M. A.
Dub. Citizen.
IX: 250.
1844. Same as 1823, *Democratic Rev.*
XV: 47. N. Y. 1844. *Lay of the Impris-
oned Knight,* H. M. M. *Colum bian
Mag.* XV: 47. N. Y. 1845. *The fairest
Flower,* (Martin.) *Blackwood's Mag.*
XLV:168. Edin. 1845. Same as 1836,
Mangan's *Ger. Anthology.* Dub. 1853.
The Beauteous Flower, Bowring.
Poems. Lond.
1855. *My Favorite Flower,* M. A. Burt.
Specimens etc.
Lond., Leip.
1855. *The Lay of the Captive Count,* A.
C. Kendricks.
Poems. Lond., N. Y., Chic.
1859. Same as 1845, Aytoun-Martin.
Poems. Lond.,
N. Y.
1859. *The Beautiful Flower,* Thomas.
Poems. Phil.
111. *Ritter Kurts Brautfahrt.*
1853. *Sir Kurt's Wedding Journey,*
Bowring. Poems.
Lond.
112. *Hochzeitlied.*
1848. *A Lay of Christmas,* Percy Boyd.
Ballads, etc.
Dublin.
1848. Same version, *Dub. Univ. Mag.*
XXXI: 305.
1853. *Wedding Song,* Bowring. Poems.
Lond.,
1859. *An Autumn Night's Dream,* Ay-
toun-Martin.
Poems. Lond., N. Y.

113. *Der Schatzgrdber.*
1835. *The Treasure Seeker,* (J. C. Mangan.) *Dub.
Univ. Mag.* V:406.
1839. *The Treasure Digger,* Dwight.
Poems. Bost.
1844. *The Treasure Digger,* (Aytoun.)
*Blackwood's
Mag.* LVI: 423. Edin.
1845. Same as 1835, Mangan's *Ger. Anthology.* Dublin.
1853. *The Treasure Digger,* A.
Baskerville. *Poetry of
Ger.* Lond., N. Y., Phil., Leip.
1853. *The Treasure Digger,* Bowring.
Poems. Lond.
1859. *The Treasure Digger,* (Anon.) *Littell's Living
Age.* LXI:186. Bost.
1859. Same as 1844, Aytoun-Martin.
Poems. Lond.,
N. Y.
1859. Same as 1844, Aytoun, *Littell's
Living Age.*
LXI:186. Bost.
114. *Der Rattenfanger.* 1841. *The Rat
Catcher,* E. B. Impey. Specimens, etc.
Lond.
1841. Same version, Sunderland's *De-
signs and Border Illustrations.* Lond.
1853. Same version, *N. Y. Lit. World.*
VII: 84.
1853. *The Rat Catcher,* Bowring.
Poems. Lond.
115. *Die Spinnerin.* 1853. *The Spinner.*
Bowring. Poems. Lond. 116. *Vor
Gericht.* 1853. *Before a Court of Jus-
tice,* Bowring. Poems. Lond. 117. *Der
Edelknabe und die Mullerin.* 1853. *The
Page and the Miller's Daughter,*
Bowring.
Poems. Lond. 1859. *The Traveller and
the Peasant Maid,* Thomas.
Poems. Phil.
118. *Der Junggeselle und der
Muhlbach.* 1839. *The Youth and the
MUlstream,* Dwight. Poems.
Bost.
1839. Same version, *Western Messen-
ger,* VI: 259.
Louisville.
1842. *The Shepherd and the Brook,*
"Wm. Falconer. *Graham's Mag.* XXI:
280. Phil. 1853. *The Youth and the Mill-
stream,* Bowring. Poems. Lond. 1859.

The Youth and the MUlstream, Aytoun-
Martm.
Poems. Lond., N. Y. 1859. *The Youth
and the Millstream,* Thomas. Poems.
Phil.
119. *Der Mullerin Verrat.* 1853. *The
Maid of the Mill's Treachery,* Bowring.
Poems. Lond. 1859. *The Treacherous
Maid of the Mill,* Aytoun-Martin.
Poems. Lond., N. Y. 120. *Der Mullerin
Reue.*
1853. *The Maid of the Mill's Repen-
tance,* Bowring.
Poems. Lond.
121. *Wandrer and Pdchterin.*
1853. *The Traveller and the Farm
Maiden,* Bowring.
Poems. Lond.
1859. *The Traveller and the Peasant
Maid,* Thomas.
Poems. Phil.
122. *Wirkung in die Feme.*
1853. *Effect at a Distance,* A.
Baskerville. *Poetry of
Germany.* Lond., N. Y., Phil., Leip.
1853. *Effect at a Distance,* Bowring.
Poems. Lond.
1859. *The Page and the Maid of Ho-
nour,* Aytoun-Martin. Poems. Lond., N.
Y.
1859. *Distant Influence,* Thomas.
Poems. Phil.
123. *Die wandelnde Qlocke.*
1850. *The Walking Bell,* C. R. Lambert.
Poems, etc.
Lond.
1853. *The Walking Bell,* Bowring.
Poems. Lond.
1859. *The Roving Boy,* Aytoun-Martin.
Poems. Lond.,
N. Y.
124. *Der getreue Eckart.*
1839. *The Trusty Eckart,* Dwight.
Poems. Bost.
1853. *Faithful Eckart,* Bowring. Poems.
Lond.
1859. *Eckart the Trusty,* (Th. Martin.)
Once A Week.
I:89. Lond.
1859. *The Trusty Eckart,* Thomas.
Poems. Phil.
125. *Der Totentanz.*
1832. *The Skeleton Dance,* H. S. *Lit.
Gazette,* p. 731.
Lond.

1836. *Dance of the Dead*, Anon. *Library of Romance.*
Lond.
1845. *Dance of Death*, (Th. Martin.) *Blackwood's Mag.*
XLV:167. Edin.
1845. *Skeleton's Dance*, J. Gostwick. *Ger. Lit.* Lond. 1853. *The Dance of Death*, Bowring. Poems. Lond. 1859. Same as 1845, Aytoun-Martin. Poems. Lond., N. Y. 1859. *The Dance of the Dead*, Thomas. Poems. Phil. 126. *Die erste Walpurgisnacht.* 1835. *The First Walpurgis Night*, J. Anster. *Faustus.*
Lond.
1853. *The First Walpurgis Night*, Bowring. Poems. Lond. 1855. *The First Walpurgis Night*, M. A. Burt. Specimens, etc. Lond. 127. *Der Zauberlehrling.* 1830. *The Apprentice to Magic*, Wm. Taylor. *Hist. Survey of Ger. Poetry.* Lond. 1831. *The Apprentice to Magic*, same version. *Amer. Quart. Rev.* X:194. Phil. 1836. *The Apprentice to Magic*, same version, Bokum. *Ger. Wreath.* Bost. 1838. *The Apprentice to Magic*, Anon. *Blackwood's Mag.* XLII:578. Edin. 1839. *The Magician's Apprentice*, Dwight, Poems.
Bost.
1839. *The Magician's Apprentice*, S. Menzies. *Court Mag.* I:117. Lond. 1841. *The Magician's Apprentice*, E. B. Impey. Specimens, etc. Lond. 1841. *The Magician's Apprentice*, J. H. Merivale, in
Sunderland's *Design and Border Illustrations.*
Lond.
1842. *The Magician's Apprentice*, same version. *Dub. Vfriv. Mag.* XIX: 331.
1843. *The Magician's Apprentice*, A. C. Kendrick, *Orion.* III: 171. Georgia.
1844. Same as 1841, Merivale. Poems translated and original. Lond. 1845. *The Magician's Apprentice*, (Th. Martin) *Black wood's Mag.* LVI:430. Edin. 1846. *The Magician's Apprentice*, Anon. *Tait's Edin.*
Mag. XIII: 99.
1853. *The Pupil in Magic*, Bowring. Poems. Lond.
1855. *The Apprentice in Magic*, A. C. Kendrick.
Echoes, etc. N. Y., Chic, Rochester. Not

the
same version as 1843.
1859. Same as 1845, Aytoun-Martin. Poems. Lond.,
N. Y.
1859. *The Wizard's Apprentice.* Thomas. Poems. Phil.
128. *Die Braut von Korinth.*
1819. *The Bride of Corinth*, Anon. *Blackwood's Mag.*
IV: 688. Edin.
1830. *The Vampire Nun*, Wm. Taylor. *Historic Survey*
of German Poetry. Lond.
1835. *The Bride of Corinth*, J. Anster. *Faustus.* Lond.
1836. *The Bride of Corinth*, J. J. Campbell. *Song of*
the Bell. Edin.
1844. *The Bride of Corinth*, (Aytoun-Martin) *Black-*
wood's Magazine. LVI:57. Edin.
1853. *The Bride of Corinth*, Bowring. Poems. Lond.
1859. Same as 1844, Aytoun-Martin. Poems. Lond.,
N. Y.
129. *Der Gott und die Bajadere. Indische Legende.*
1809. *The Genius and the Bay der e*, Anon. (Sir Brooke
Boothy.) *Edin. Annual Register.* II:647.
1813. *The Genius and the Baydere*, same version. *Poly-*
anthus. II: 161. Bost.
1825. *Indian God and the Bayadeer*, Anon. *N. T. Rev.*
and Athenaeum. I:165.
1827. *The God and the Bayadere*, C. Des Voeux. *Tasso,*
etc. Lond.
1844. *The God and the Bayadere*, (Aytoun-Martin)
Blackwood's Mag. LVT:421. Edin.
1853. *The God and the Bayadere*, Bowring. Poems.
Lond.
1859. *The God and the Bayadere*, Aytoun-Martin.
Poems. Lond., N. Y.
ELEGIEN. I.
ROEMISCHE ELEGIEN.
130. I. *Saget, Steine, mir an.* 1853. A. Baskerville. *Spirit of Ger. Poetry.* Lond.
, N.

Y., Phil., Leip.
1853. Bowring. Poems. Lond.
1859. Thomas. Poems. Phil.
131. III. *Lass dich, Geliebte, nicht reun.*
1846. *Blackwood's Mag.* LIX: 120. Edin.
1853. Bowring. Poems. Lond.
1855. Th. Martin, in Lewes' *Life of Goethe.* Lond.,
Bost.
1859. Thomas. Poems. Phil. 132. VIII. *Wenn du mir sagst.* 1855. G. H. Lewes, in *Life of Goethe.* Lond., Bost. 133. X. *Alexander and Cdsar und Heinrich.* 1830. Wm. Taylor. *Historic Survey of Ger. Poetry.* Lond. 1853. Bowring. Poems. Lond. 134. XL *Euch, o Grazien.* 1853. Bowring. Poems. Lond. 135. XIII. *Amor bleibet ein Schalk.* 1853. Bowring. Poems. Lond. 136. XVII. *Manche Tone sind mir Verdruss.* 1833. Mrs. Sarah Austin. *Goethe's Characteristics.* I:252. Lond.
1853. Thomas. Poems. Phil.
ELEGIEN. H. 137. *Alexis und Dora.* 1829. Anon. *Athenaeum.* II: 677. Lond.
1842. C. P. Cranch in Brooks' *Songs and Ballads.*
Lond., Bost.
1847. (J. C. Hare.) *Eng. Hexameter Translations* etc.
Lond.
1849. Anon. *Democratic Rev.* XXIV: 66. N. Y.
1853. Bowring. Poems. Lond.
138. *Euphrosyne.* 1833. Prose translation, 12 lines, Mrs. Sarah Austin. *Goethe's Characteristics.* I:160. Lond.
139. *Die Metamorphose der Pflanzen.* 1833. Mrs. Sarah Austin. *Goethe's Characteristics.* I:167. Lond.
1839. Dwight. Poems. Bost.
1847. (J. C. Hare.) *Eng. Hexameter Translations.*
Lond.
1853. Bowring. Poems. Lond. 1859. Wm. Whewell. *History of Inductive Science.* III:360. Lond. 140. *Erste Epistel.* 1829. *Poetical Epistle*, J. C. H(are?) *Athenaeum.* II:261. Lond. 141. *Zweite Epistel.* 1829. *Second Poetical Epistle*, J. C. H(are?) *Athen aeum.* II: 297. Lond. 142. *Epigramme. Venedig. 1790.* 1830. Wm. Taylor. *Historic Survey of Ger. Poetry.*
Lond. (8 and 34b.) 1833. Mrs. Sarah

Austin. *Goethe's Characteristics.* Lond. (34b, 73, 98.) 1838. (Anon.) *Western Messenger.* IV: 379. Louisville. (12.) 1839. Dwight. Poems. Boat. (8, 12, 15, 22, 34b, 50, 55, 57, 58, 59, 61, 62, 75.) 1846. (Anon.) *Blackwood's Mag.* LIX:120. Edin.
(96.) 1853. Bowring. Poems. Lond. (1, 8, 10, 14, 35, 46, 88, 89, 94, 95, 96, 97.) 143. *Weissagungen des Bakis.* 1839. *Prophecies of Bakis,* (5 stanzas) Dwight. Poems. Bost. (VOL. II) SONETTE. 144. I. *Mächtiges Veberraschen.* 1837. Bettina von Arnim. *Goethe's Correspondence with a Child.* p. 89. Lond. 145. II. *Freundliches Begegnen.* 1853. *The Friendly Meeting,* Bowring. Poems. Lond. 1859. *The Friendly Meeting,* Thomas, Poems. Phil. 146. III. *Kurz und gut.* 1853. *In a Word,* Bowring. Poems. Lond. 1859. *The Resolution,* Thomas. Poems. Phil.
147. IV. *Das Mädchen spricht.* 1837. Bettina von Arnim. *Goethe's Correspondence with a Child.* p. 487. Lond. 1853. *The Maiden Speaks,* Bowring. Poems. Lond. 1859. *The Maiden Speaks,* Thomas. Poems. Phil. 148. V. *Wachstum.* 1837. Bettina von Arnim. *Goethe's Correspondence with a Child.* p. 487. Lond. 1853. *Growth,* Bowring. Poems. Lond. 1859. *Growth,* Thomas. Poems. Phil. 149. VI. *Reisezehrung.* 1853. *Food in Travel,* Bowring. Poems. Lond. 150. VII. *Abschied.* 1837. Bettina von Arnim. *Goethe's Correspondence* *with a Child.* p. 89. Lond. 1853. *Departure,* Bowring. Poems. Lond.
151. VIII. *Die Liebende schreibt.* 1837. Bettina von Arnim. *Goethe's Correspondence* *with a Child,* p. 500. Lond. 1853. *The Loving One Writes,* Bowring. Poems. Lond. 1859. *She Writes,* Thomas. Poems. Phil. 152. IX. *Die Liebende abermals.* 1837. Bettina von Arnim. *Goethe's Correspondence* *with a Child.* p. 500. Lond. 1853. *The Loving One Once More,* Bowring. Poems. Lond.

1859. *She Writes Again,* Thomas. Poems. Phil.
153. X. *Sie kann nicht enden.* 1837. Bettina von Arnim. *Goethe's Correspondence* *with a Child.* p. 502. Lond. 1853. *She Cannot End,* Bowring. Poems. Lond.
1859. *She Cannot Cease,* Thomas. Poems. Phil.
154. XL *Nemesis.* 1853. *Nemesis,* Bowring. Poems. Lond. 155. XII. *Christgeschenk.* 1853. *The Christmas Box,* Bowring. Poems. Lond.
156. XIII. *Warnung.* 1853. *The Warning,* Bowring. Poems. Lond. 1856. *The Warning, W. B. Rands. Twit's Edin. Mag.* XXIII: 238. 1859. *Warning,* Thomas. Poems. Phil.
157. XIV. *Die Zweifelnden und die Liebenden.* 1853. *The Doubters and the Lovers,* Bowring. Poems. Lond.
158. XVI. *Epoche.* 1837. Bettina von Arnim. *Goethe's Correspondence with a Child.* p. 70. Lond. 1853. *The Epochs,* Bowring. Poems. Lond.
159. XVII. *Charade.* 1837. Bettina von Arnim. *Goethe's Correspondence with a Child.* p. 179. Lond. 1853. *Charade,* Bowring. Poems. Lond.
KANTATEN 160. *Deutscher Parnass.* 1853. *The German Parnassus,* Bowring. Poems. Lond. 161. *Idylle.* 1853. *Idyll.* Bowring. Poems. Lond. 162. *Johanna Sebus.* 1853. *Johanna Sebus,* Bowring. Poems. Lond. 163. *Rinaldo.* 1853. *Rinaldo,* Bowring. Poems. Lond. VEEMISCHTE GEDICHTE 164. *Klaggesang von der edlen Frauen des Asan Aga.* 1799. *Morlachian Ballad,* Walter Scott. (Privately printed with an apology, intended for M. G. Lewis' *Tales of Terror.* It is not included in Scott's collected works.) 1836. *Hassan Aga,* (J. C. Mangan.) *Dub. TJniv. Mag.* VII: 495. 1844. *Doleful Lay of the Wife of Asan Aga,* (Aytoun.) *Blackwood's Mag.* LVI:67. Edin. 1845. Same as 1836, Mangan's *Ger. Anthology.* Dub.

Goedeke's *Grundriss,* §236: 126, mentions a translation of this poem In the *Westminster Review,* VI: 23. 1826, London, but It is not a translation, only an outline of the story of the ballad In prose. 1853. *Death Lament of the Noble Wife of Asan Aga.* Bowring. Poems. Lond. 1854. *Lament of Hassan Aga's Noble Wife.* M. A. Burt. Specimens etc. Lond.
1855. *Mournful History of the Noble Wife of Asan Ago,* G. Bancroft. *Lit. and Hist. Miscellanies.* N. Y.
1859. Same as 1844, Aytoun-Martin. Poems. Lond., N. Y.
165. *Mahomets Gesang.* 1800. *Mahomet,* Anon. *German Museum.* Lond. 1830. *Mahomet's Song,* Win. Taylor. *Hist. Survey of Ger. Poetry.* Lond. 1839. *Mahomet's Song,* Dwight. Poems. Bost. 1845. Same version, in Longfellow's *Poets of Europe.* Lond., Phil. 1845. *Mahomet's Song,* (J. Anster.) *Dub. Univ. Mag.* XXV: 156. 1853. *Mahomet's Song,* Bowring. Poems. Lond. 1853. *Mahomet's Song,* (Martin.) *Fraser's Mag.* XLVIII:114. Lond. 1859. Same version, Aytoun-Martin. Poems. N. Y.
166. *Gesang der Geister iiber den Wassern.* 1839. *Song of the Spirits over the Water,* Dwight. Poems. Bost. 1845. Same version, in Longfellow's *Poets of Europe.* Lond.,-Phil. 1853. *Spirit Song over Waters,* Bowring. Poems. Lond. 1859. *Song of the Spirits over the Waters,* (Th. Martin) *Fraser's Mag.* LIX: 712. Lond. 1859. Same version. Aytoun-Martin. Poems. Lond.,

N. Y.

167. *Meine Gottin.*

1824. *My Goddess*, G. Bancroft. TV. *Amer. Rev.* XIX: 308. Bost.

1839. Same version, in Dwight's Poems. Bost.

1839. *My Goddess*, Dwight. Poems. Bost. (Dwight prints two versions, his own and Bancroft's.)

1853. *My Goddess*, Bowring. Poems. Lond.

1855. Same as 1824, Bancroft. *Lit. and Hist. Miscel-lanies.* N. Y.

168. *Harzreise im Winter.*

1839. *Ride to the Harz in Winter*, Dwight. Poems. Bost.

1853. *Winter Journey over the Harz*, Bowring. Poems. Lond.

169. *An Schwager Kronos.*

1853. *To Father Kronos*, Bowring. Poems. Lond.

170. *Wandrers Sturmlied.*

1853. *The Wanderer's Storm Song*, Bowring. Poems. Lond.

171. *Seefahrt.*

1853. *The Sea Voyage*, Bowring. Poems. Lond.

172. *Adler und Taube.*

1824. *Eagle and Dove*, G. Bancroft. JV. *Amer. Rev.* XIX: 323. Bost.

1839. *Eagles and Doves*, Margaret Fuller, in Dwight's Poems. Bost.

1853. *The Eagle and the Dove*, Bowring. Poems. Lond.

1855. Same as 1839, in *Life Within and Without*, p. 387. Bost.

173. *Prometheus.*

1802. *Prometheus*, Henry Crabb Robinson. *Lit. Re-mains.* Lond.

1833. *Prometheus*, Mrs. Sarah Austin. *Goethe's Char-acteristics.* I:262. Lond.

1838. *Prometheus*, Margaret Fuller. Boat. (Not pub-lished.)

1839. *Prometheus*, Dwight. Poems.

Bost.

1844. *Prometheus*, (Th. Martin.) *Black-wood's Mag.* LVI:428. Edin.

1845. Same as 1839, in Longfellow's *Poets of Europe.* Lond., Phil.

1846. *Prometheus*, (Anon.) *Tait's Edin. Mag.* XIII: 98.

1850. Same as 1844, *Dub. Univ. Mag.* XXXVI: 529. (Contains the entire fragment.)

1852. *Prometheus*, Mrs. Haller. Trans-lations, etc. Lond.

1853. *Prometheus*, Bowring. Poems. Lond.

1855. *Prometheus*, G. H. Lewes, *Life of Goethe.* Lond., Bost.

1859. Same as 1844, Aytoun-Martin. Poems. Lond., N. Y.

174. *Ganymed.*

1839. *Ganymede*, Dwight. Poems. Bost.

1853. *Ganymede*, Bowring. Poems. Lond.

1859. *Ganymede*, Aytoun-Martin. Poems. Lond., N. Y.

175. *Grenzen der Menschheit.*

1839. *Limits of Man*, Dwight. Poems. Bost.

1853. *Boundaries of Humanity*, Bowring. Poems. Lond.

1859. *Limits of Humanity*, Aytoun-Martin. Poems. Lond., N. Y.

1859. Same version, *Fraser's Mag.* LIX:711. Lond.

176. *Das Gottliche.*

1839. *The Godlike*, G. Bancroft, in Dwight's Poems. Bost.

1839. Same version, *N. Amer. Rev.* XLVIII:510. Bost.

1839. *The Godlike*, Dwight. Poems. Bost.

1839. Same version, *N. Amer. Rev.* XLVIII:510. Bost.

Braun, F. A., *Margaret Fuller and Goethe*, pp. 215-237, Holt & Co., N. T., 1910.

1841. *The Godlike*, Margaret Fuller. *The Dial.* I: 344. Bost.

1853. *The Godlike*, Bowring. Poems. Lond.

1859. Same as 1841, in *Life Within and Without*, p. 18, Bost.

177. *Koniglich Gebet.*

1853. *Royal Prayer*, Bowring. Poems. Lond.

178. *Menschengefiihl.*

1853. *Human Feelings*, Bowring. Poems. Lond.

179. *LiUsPark.*

1833. *Lili's Park*, Mrs. Sarah Austin. *Goethe's Char-acteristics.* I:279. Lond.

1853. *Lili's Menagerie*, Bowring. Poems. Lond.

1859. *Lili's Menagerie*, Aytoun-Martin. Poems. Lond., N. Y.

1859. *Lili's Menagerie*, Thomas. Poems. Phil.

180. *Liebebediirfnis.*

1853. *Love's Distresses.* Bowring. Poems. Lond.

1859. *Chapped Lips*, Thomas. Poems. Phil.

181. *Siisse Sorgen.*

1852. *Sweet Cares*, Mrs. Haller. Trans-lations, etc. Lond

182. *Anliegen.*

1853. *Petition*, Bowring. Poems. Lond.

183. *An seine Sprdde.*

1853. *To his Coy One*, Bowring. Poems. Lond.

184. *Die Musageten.*

1853. *The Musagetes*, Bowring. Poems. Lond.

1859. *The Musagetes*, Aytoun-Martin. Poems. Lond., N. Y.

185. *Morgenklagen.*

1853. *Morning Lament*, Bowring. Poems. Lond.

186. *Der Besuch.*

1845. *The Visit*, "Horus." Imitated from Goethe. *Amer. Whig Rev.* I:289. N. Y.

1853. *The Visit*, Bowring. Poems. Lond.

1853. Same version, *Lond. Examiner.*

1853. Same version,*Littell's Living Age.* XXXVIII: 123. Bost.

1859. *The Visit*, Aytoun-Martin. Poems. Lond., N. Y.

187. *Magisches Netz.*
1853. *The Magic Net, Bowring.* Poems. Lond.
188. *Der Becker.*
1853. *The Goblet,* Bowring. Poems. Lond.
1859. *The Goblet,* Aytoun-Martin. Poems. Lond., N. Y.
189. *Nachtgedanken.*
1827. *Night Thoughts,* C. Des Voeux. *Tasso,* etc. Lond.
1830. *Night Thoughts,* "Yorke." *Fraser's Mag.* I:216. Lond.
1844. *Night Thoughts,* (Th. Martin.) *Blackwood's Mag.* LVI:428. Edin.
1853. *Night Thoughts,* Bowring. Poems. Lond.
1859. *Night Thoughts,* Thomas. Poems. Phil.
1859. Same as 1844, Aytoun-Martin. Poems. Lond., N. Y.
190. *An Lida.*
1853. *To Lida,* Bowring. Poems. Lond.
1859. *To Lida,* Thomas. Poems. Phil.
191. *Nahe.*
1853. *Proximity.* Bowring. Poems. Lond.
1859. *Nearness,* Thomas. Poems. Phil.
192. *An die Cicade.*
1853. *To the Grasshopper,* Bowring. Poems. Lond.
AUS WILHELM MEISTEB
193. *Heiss mich nicht reden.*
1824. Thomas Carlyle, in *Wilhelm Meistev.* Lond., Edin.
1855. R. D. Doylan, in *Wilhelm Meister.* Lond.
1859. "Nominis Umbra." Lond.
1859. Thomas. Poems. Phil.
194. *Nur wer die Sehnsucht kennt.*
1824. Thos. Carlyle, *Wilhelm Meister.* Lond., Edin.
1853. Bowring, Poems. Lond.
1855. R. D. Boylan. *Wilhelm Meister.* Lond.
1859. Thomas. Poems. Phil.
195. *So lasst mich scheinen*
1824. Thos. Carlyle. *Wilhelm Meister.* Lond. Edin.
1852. Mrs. Haller. Translations, etc. Lond.

1855. R. D. Boylan. *Wilhelm Meister.* Lond.
1859. Thomas. Poems. Phil.
196. *Wer sich der Einsamkeit etfgibt.*
1824. Thos. Carlyle. *Wilhelm Meister.* Lond., Edin.
1836. J. J. Campbell. *Song of the Bell.* etc. Lond.
1853. Bowring. Poems. Lond.
1855. R. D. Boylan. *Wilhelm Meister.* Lond.
1859. Thomas. Poems. Phil.
197. *An die Tiiren will ich schleichen.*
1824. Thos. Carlyle. *Wilhelm Meister.* Lond. Edin.
1855. R. D. Boylan. *Wilhelm Meister.* Lond.
1859. Thomas. Poems. Phil.
198. *Wer nie sein Brot mit Tranen ass.*
1824. Thos. Carlyle. *Wilhelm Meister.* Lond., Edin.
1845. (Th. Martin.) *Blackwood's Mag.* LVT:175. Edin.
1852. Mrs. Haller» Translations, etc. Lond.
1853. Bowring. Poems. Lond.
1855. R. D. Boylan. *Wilhelm Meister.* Lond.
1856. (Anon.) *Blackwood's Mag.* LXXX:416. Edin.
1859. Carlyle's version, *Fraser's Mag.* LIX:713. Lond.
1859. A. H. Clough, *Fraser's Mag.* LIX: 713. Lond.
1859. Martin's version, *Fraser's Mag.* LIX: 713. Lond.
1859. Martin's version, *Littell's Living Age.* LXI: 184. Bost.
1859. Martin's version, Aytoun-Martin. Poems. Lond., N. y.
1859. Thomas. Poems. Phil.
199. *PMine.*
1824. Thos. Carlyle. *Wilhelm Meister.* Lond., Edin.
1844. (Th. Martin.) *Blackwood's Mag.* LVI:426. Edin.
1853. Bowring. Poems. Lond.
1855. R. D. Boylan. *Wilhelm Meister.* Lond.
1856. (Anon.) *Blackwood's Mag.* LXXX:420. Edin.

1859. Aytoun-Martin. Poems. Lond., N. Y.
1859. Thomas. Poems. Phil.
ANTIKER FORM SICH NAEHERND
200. *Herzog Leopold von Braunschweig.*
1853. *Leopold, Duke of Brunswick,* Bowring. Poems. Lond.
201. *Dern, Ackermann.*
1820. *To the Husbandman,* (Anon.) *Scots Mag.* VI: 329. Edin. (Possibly Wm. Taylor.)
1845. *The Husbandman,* (Th. Martin.) *Blackwood's Mag.* LVII:175. Edin.
1853. *The Husbandman,* Bowring. Poems. Lond.
1859. Same as 1845, Aytoun-Martin. Poems. Lond., N. Y.
202. *Anakreons Grab.*
1845. *Anacreon's Grave,* (Aytoun.) *Blackwood's Mag.* LVII:175. Edin.
1846. *Anacreon's Grave,* ("P. M.".) *Blackwood's Mag.* LIX:121. Edin.
1853. *Anacreon's Grave,* Bowring. Poems. Lond.
1859. *Anacreon's Grave,* Thomas. Poems. Phil.
1859. Same as 1845, Aytoun-Martin. Poems. Lond., N. Y.
203. *Die Geschwister.*
1845. *The Brothers,* (Aytoun.) *Blackwood's Mag.* LVII:176. Edin.
1853. *The Brethren,* Bowring. Poems. Lond.
1859. *The Brothers,* Thomas. Poems. Phil.
1859. Same as 1845, Aytoun-Martin. Poems. Lond., N. Y.
1859. Same as 1845, *Fraser's Mag.* LIX:716. Lond.
204. *Zeitmass.*
1845. *Love's Hour Glass,* (Aytoun.) *Blackwood's Mag.* LVII:176. Edin.
1853. *Measure of Time,* Bowring. Poems. Lond.
1859. Same as 1845, Aytoun-Martin.

Poems. Lond.,
N. Y.

205. *Warming.* (Wecke den Amor nicht auf)
1845. *Warning,* (Aytoun.) *Blackwood's Mag.*
LVII:176. Edin.
1846. *Warning,* (P. M.) *Blackwood's Mag.* LIX:121.
Edin.
1853. *Warning,* Bowring. Poems. Lond.
1859. *Warning,* Thomas. Poems. Phil.
1859. Same as 1845, Aytoun-Martin. Poems. Lond.,
N. Y.

206. *Einsamkeit.*
1845. *Solitude,* (Th. Martin.) *Blackwood's Mag.*
LVII:176. Edin.
1853. *Solitude,* Bowring. Poems. Lond.
1859. Same as 1845. Aytoun-Martin. Poems. Lond.,
N. Y.

207. *Erkanntes Gliick.*
1845. *Perfect Bliss.* (Th. Martin.) *Blackwood's Mag.*
LVII:176. Edin.
1859. Same version. Aytoun-Martin. Poems. Lond.,
N. Y.

208. *Erwdhlter Fels.*
1845. *The Chosen Rock,* (Th. Martin.) *Blackwood's Mag.* LVII:177. Edin.
1853. *The Chosen Cliff,* Bowring. Poems. Lond.
1859. *The Chosen Stone,* Thomas. Poems. Phil.
1859. Same as 1845. Aytoun-Martin. Poems. Lond.,
N. Y.

209. *Philomele.*
1845. *Philomela,* (Th. Martin.) *Blackwood's Mag.*
LVII:177. Edin.
1859. *Philomela,* Thomas. Poems. Phil.
1859. Same as 1845, Aytoun-Martin. Poems. Lond.,
N. Y.

210. *Geweihter Platz.*
1845. *Sacred Ground,* (Aytoun.) *Blackwood's Mag.*
LVII:177. Edin.
1853. *The Consecrated Spot,* Bowring. Poems. Lond.

1859. Same as 1845, Aytoun-Martin. Poems. Lond.,
N. Y.

211. *DerPark.*
1845. *The Park,* (Th. Martin.) *Blackwood's Mag.*
LVII: 178. Edin.
1859. Same version, Aytoun-Martin. Poems. Lond.,
N. Y.

212. *Die Lehrer.*
1845. *The Teachers,* (Th. Martin.) *Blackwood's Mag.*
LVII: 178. Edin.
1855. *The Instructors,* Bowring. Poems. Lond.
1859. Same as 1845, Aytoun-Martin. Poems. Lond.,
N. Y.
1859. Same as 1845, *Fraser's Mag.* LIX: 716. Lond.

213. *Ungleiche Heirat.*
1845. *Marriage Unequal,* (Aytoun.) *Blackwood's Mag.*
LVII:178. Edin.
1853. *The Unequal Marriage,* Bowring. Poems. Lond.
1859. Same as 1845, Aytoun-Martin. Poems. Lond.,
N. Y.

214. *Die heilige Familie.*
1845. *The Holy Family,* (Aytoun.) *Blackwood's Mag.*
LVII: 178. Edin.
1859. Same version. Aytoun-Martin. Poems. Lond.,
N. Y.
1859. Same version, *Fraser's Mag.* LIX: 716. Lond.

215. *Entschuldigung.*
1814. *Inconstancy,* Anon. *L. Mo. Mag.* XXXVII: 146.
Lond. (Possibly Wm. Taylor.)
1845. *Exculpation,* (Aytoun.) *Blackwood's Mag.*
LVII: 179. Edin.
1846. *Epigram,* (Anon.) *Haileybury Observer. IV: 81.*
Hartford.
1853. *Excuse,* Bowring. Poems. Lond.
1859. *Excuse,* Thomas. Poems. Phil.
1859. Same as 1845. Aytoun-Martin. Poems. Lond.,
N. Y.
1859. Same as 1845, *Fraser's Mag.* LIX:

715. Lond.
216. *Der Chinese in Rom.*
1859. *The Chinaman in Rome,* Aytoun-Martin. Poems.
Lond., N. Y.
1859. *The Chinese in Rome,* Thomas. Poems. Phil.

217. *Spiegel der Muse.*
1845. *The Muse's Mirror,* (Th. Martin.) *Blackwood's Mag.* LVII:179. Edin.
1853. *The Muse's Mirror,* Bowring. Poems. Lond.
1859. Same as 1845, Aytoun-Martin. Poems. Lond.,
N. Y.

218. *Phbbus und Hermes.*
1845. *Phoebus and Hermes,* (Th. Martin.) Blackwood's Mag. LVII:179. Edin.
1853. *Phoebus and Hermes,* Bowring. Poems. Lond.
1859. Same as 1845, Aytoun-Martin. Poems. Lond.,
N. Y.
1859. Same as 1845, *Fraser's Mag.* LIX: 715. Lond.

219. *Der neue Amor.*
1845. *A New Love,* (Th. Martin.) *Blackwood's Mag.*
LVII:179. Edin.
1859. *The New Amor* Bowring. Poems. Lond.
1859. Same as 1845, Aytoun-Martin. Poems. Lond.,
N. Y.

220. *Hie Kranze.*
1845. *The Wreaths,* (Aytoun-Martin.) *Blackwood's Mag.* LVII:180. Edin.
1853. *The Garlands,* Bowring. Poems. Lond.
1859. Same as 1845, Aytoun-Martin. Poems. Lond.,
N. Y.

221. *Schweizeralpe.*
1845. *The Swiss Alp,* (Aytoun.) *Blackwood's Mag*
LVII: 180. Edin.
1846. *The Swiss Alp,* P. M. *Blackwood's Mag.* LIX: 120.
Edin.
1853. *The Swiss Alps,* Bowring. Poems. Lond.
1859. Same as 1845, Aytoun-Martin.

Poems. Lond.,
N. Y.
1859. Same as 1845, *Fraser's Mag.* LIX:
715. Lond.

AN PERSONEN

222. *Gellert's Monument von Oeser.*
1859. *Gellert's Monument by Oeser,*
Thomas. Poems.
Phil.

KUNST

223. *Die Nektartropfen.*
1802. *Drops of Nectar,* Anon. *L. Mo.
Mag.* II: 26. (Possibly We Taylor.)
Lond.
1853. *The Drops of Nectar,* Bowring.
Poems. Lond.
1853. *The Drops of Nectar,* Thomas.
Poems. Phil.
1859. *The Nectar Drops,* Aytoun-
Martin. Poems.
Lond., N. Y.

224. *Der Wandrer.*
1798. *The Wanderer,* (Wm. Taylor.) *L.
Mo. Mag.*
VI: 120.
1798. Same version, *Scots Mag.* LX:
627. Edin.
1820. Same version, *Scots Mag.* New
series, VI: 331.
Edin.
1830. Same version, Taylor's *Hist. Survey of Ger.
Poetry.* Lond.
1831. Same version, *Amer. Quart. Rev.*
X: 194. Phil.
1836. Same version, Bokum's *Ger.
Wreath.* Bost.
1839. *The Wanderer,* Dwight. Poems.
Bost.
1845. *The Wanderer,* Anon. *Godey's
Lady's Book.*
XXXI: 265. Phil., N. Y.
1848. *The Wanderer,* C. L. L. *South. Lit.
Messenger.*
XIV: 420. Richmond, Va.
1853. *The Wanderer,* Bowring. Poems.
Lond.
1859. *The Wanderer,* Aytoun-Martin.
Poems. Lond.,
N. Y.

225. *Kunstlers Morgenlied.*
1844. *Artist's Morning Song,* (Martin.)
*Blackwood's
Mag.* LVI: 419. Edin.
1859. Same version, Aytoun-Martin.

Poems. Lond
N. Y.
226. *Amor als Landschaftsmaler.*
1802. *Cupid as Landscape Painter,*
(Anon.) *Mo. Regis-
ter.* II:26. Lond.
1839. *Cupid as Landscape Painter, G.*
Bancroft, in
Dwight's Poems. Bost.
1839. *Cupid as Landscape Painter,* S.
Naylor. A Drama,
etc. Maidenhead. Eng.
1844. *Cupid as Landscape Painter,*
(Aytoun) *Black-
wood's Mag.* LVI: 417. Edin.
1853. *Love as Landscape Painter,*
Bowring. Poems.
Lond.
1859. *Amor as Landscape Painter,* "Nominis Umbra."
Lond.
1859. Same as 1844, Aytoun-Martin.
Poems. Lond.,
N. y.

227. *Kiinstlers Abendlied.*
1839. *Artist's Evening Song,* Dwight.
Poems. Bost.

228. *GuterRat.*
1828. *Good Advice,* F. Page, in *Employment.* Bath,
Eng.

229. *Gross ist die Diana der Epheser.*
1845. *The Goldsmith of Ephesus,* J.
Gostwick. *Spirit
of Ger. Poetry.* Lond.

PARABOLISCH

230. *Erkldrung einer antiken Gemme.*
1853. *Explanation of an Antique Gem,*
Bowring. Poems.
Lond.

231. *Katzenpastete.*
1853. *Cat Pie,* Bowring. Poems. Lond.

232. *Legende.* (In der Wiisten ein
heiliger Mann)
1853. *Legend,* Bowring. Poems. Lond.
1859. *Legend,* Thomas. Poems. Phil.

233. *Autoren.*
1836. *Authors,* (J. C. Mangan.) *Dub.
Univ. Mag.*
VII: 300.
1853. *Authors,* Bowring. Poems. Lond.

234. *Recensent.*
1836. *The Reviewer,* (Anon.) *Blackwood's Mag.*
XIII: 526. Edin.

1853. *The Critic,* Bowring. Poems.
Lond.

235. *Dilettant und Kritiker.*
1853. *The Dilettante and the Critic,*
Bowring. Poems.
Lond.

236. *Neologen.*
1836. *An Incident,* (J. C. Mangan) *Dub.
Univ. Mag.*
VII: 299.

237. *Krittler.*
1853. *The Wrangler,* Bowring. Poems.
Lond.

238. *Klaffer.*
1853. *The Yelpers,* Bowring. Poems.
Lond.

239. *Celebritat.*
1853. *Celebrity,* Bowring. Poems.
Lond.

240. *Parabel. (Pfaffenspiel.)*
1853. *Playing at Priest,* Bowring.
Poems. Lond.

GOTT, GEMUET UND WELT

241. *Gereimte Distichen, iiber funfzig.*
1803. *Mo. Register.* II: 492. Lond.
1839. Dwight. Poems. Bost. (The two
connected
with *Prooemion;* see no. 288.)
1853. *Rhymed Distichs* (nine numbers),
Bowring.
Poems. Lond.

SPRICHWOERTLICH

242. *Sprichwdrtlich.*
1839. *Proverbs,* (26) Dwight. Poems.
Boat.
1839. Same version, (5) *Western Messenger.* VII: 128.
Louisville.
1853. *Proverbs,* (5) Bowring. Poems.
Lond.
1859. *Proverbs,* (11), Thomas. Poems.
Phil.

EPIGRAMMATISCH

243. *Das garstige Gesicht.*
1859. *The Ugly Face,* Thomas. Poems.
Phil.

244. *Soldatentrost.*
1853. *Soldier's Consolation,* Bowring.
Poems. Lond.

245. *Problem.*
1839. *Memento,* Dwight. Poems. Bost.
1839. Same version, *Western Messenger.* VII: 113.
Louisville.

246. *Genialisch Treiben.*

1853. *Genial Impulse*, Bowring. Poems. Lond.

247. *Gesellschaft.*

1837. *Society*, Anon. *Western Messenger*. IV: 334.
   Louisville.

1839. *Society*, Dwight. Poems. Bost.

1859. *Society*, Thomas. Poems. Phil.

248. *Den Originalen.*

1839. *The Original*, Dwight. Poems. Bost.

1846. *An Original*, Anon. *Haileybury Observer.*
IV: 81. Hartford.

1853. *To Originals*, Bowring. Poems. Lond.

1859. *An Original*, Thomas. Poems. Phil.

249. *Den Zudringlichen.*

1859. *To the Obtrusive*, Thomas. Poems. Phil.

250. *Den Guten.*

1839. *The Good*, Dwight. Poems. Bost.

1839. Same version, *Western Messenger*. VII: 326.
Louisville.

251. *Lahmung.*

1839. *Laming*, Dwight. Poems. Bost.

252. *Spruch, Widerspruch.*

1839. *Speech, Counterspeech*, Dwight. Poems. Bost.

1859. *Contradiction*, Thomas. Poems. Phil.

253. *Demut.*

1840. *Humility*, Anon. *Dial*. I: 216. Bost., Lond.

1859. *Humility*, Thomas. Poems. Phil.

254. *Keins von alien.*

1839. *Neither of All*, Dwight. Poems. Bost.

1853. *Neither This nor That*, Bowring. Poems. Lond.

1859. *None of All*, Thomas. Poems. Phil.

255. *Lebensart.*

1853. *The Way to Behave*. Bowring. Poems. Lond.

1859. *Behavior*, Thomas. Poems. Phil.

256. *Bedingung.*

1839. *Condition*. Dwight. Poems. Bost.

1859. *Stipulation*, Thomas. Poems. Phil.

257. *Das Beste.*

1839. *The Best*, Dwight. Poems. Bost.

1853. *The Best*, Bowring. Poems. Lond.

1859. *The Best*, Thomas. Poems. Phil.

258. *Memento.*

1839. *Memento*, Dwight. Poems. Bost.

1839. Same version, *Western Messenger*. VII: 138. Louisville.

1859. *Memento*, Thomas. Poems. Phil.

259. *Ein anderes.* (Musst nicht widerstehn dem Schicksal)

1859. *Another*, Thomas. Poems. Phil.

260. *Breit wie lang.*

1853. *As Broad as it's Long*. Bowring. Poems. Lond.

1859. *Broad as Long*. Thomas. Poems. Phil.

261. *Lebensregel.*

1839. *Rule of Life*, Dwight. Poems. Bost.

1853. *Rule of Life*, Bowring. Poems. Lond.

1859. *Rule of Life*, Thomas. Poems. Phil.

262. *Das Alter.*

1853. *Old Age*, Bowring. Poems. Lond.

263. *Grabschrift.*

1853. *Epitaph*. Bowring. Poems. Lond.

264. *Beispiel.*

1839. *Example*, Dwight. Poems. Bost.

1859. *Example*, Thomas. Poems. Phil.

265. *JJmgekehrt.*

1859. *Reversed*, Thomas. Poems. Phil.

266. *Fiirstenregel.*

1853. *Rule for Monarchs*, Bowring. Poems. Lond.

267. *Egalite.*

1859. *Equality*, Thomas. Poems. Phil.

268. *Wie du mir, so ich dir.*

1839. *As Thou Me, so I Thee*, Dwight. Poems. Bost.

1859. *Reciprocity*, Thomas. Poems. Phil.

269. *Kommt Zeit, kommt Rat.*

1839. *Comes Time, Comes Council*, Dwight. Poems. Bost.

(VOL. IU) LYRISCHES

270. *Ballade.*

1853. *Ballad of the Banished and Returning Count*, Bowring. Poems. Lond.

271. I. *Des Paria Gebet.*

1853. *The Pariah's Prayer*, Bowring. Poems. Lond.

1859. *The Pariah*, Aytoun-Martin. Poems. Lond., N. Y.

II. *Legende.*

1853. *Legende*. Bowring. Poems. Lond.

1859. *The Pariah's Legend*, Aytoun-Martin. Poems. Lond., N. Y.

III. *Dank des Paria.*

1853. *The Pariah's Thanks*, Bowring. Poems. Lond.

1859. *The Pariah's Thanksgiving*, Aytoun-Martin. Poems. Lond., N. Y.

272. *Trilogie der Leidenschaft.*
   I. *An Werther*, II. *Elegie*, III. *Aussohnung.*

1853. *Trilogy of Passion*, Bowring. Poems. Lond.

273. *Lust und Qual.*

1853. *Joy and Sorrow*, Bowring. Poems. Lond.

274. *Immer unduberall.*

1853. *Ever and Everywhere*, Bowring. Poems. Lond.

275. *Mdrz.*

1853. *March*, Bowring. Poems. Lond.

1859. *March*, Thomas. Poems. Phil.

276. *April.*

1853. *April*, Bowring. Poems. Lond.

1859. *April* or *Speaking Eyes*, Thomas. Poems. Phil.

277. *Mai.*

1853. *May*. Bowring. Poems. Lond.

278. *Juni.*

1853. *June*, Bowring. Poems. Lond.

279. *Friihling iibers Jdhr.*

1853. *Next Year's Spring*. Bowring. Poems. Lond.

—. *Furs Leben.*
See no. 84, *Die gliicklichen Gotten.*

280. *Fur ewig.*

1839. *Forever*, J. F. Clarke, in Dwight's Poems. Bost.

1853. *Forever*, Bowring. Poems. Lond.

1859. *Forever*, Thomas. Poems. Phil.

281. *Aus einem Stammbuch von 1604.*

1853. *From an Album of 1604*, Bowring. Poems. Lond.

282. *Um Mitternacht.* (Um Mitternacht ging ich)

1839. *At Dead of Night*. Dwight. Poems. Bost.

1853. *At Midnight Hour*, Bowring. Poems. Lond.

1856. *At Dead of Night*, Anon. *National Rev.* II: 60.
   Lond.

1856. Same version, *Littell's Living Age.* L: 29. Bost.
283. *Gegenseitig.*
1853. *Reciprocal,* Bowring. Poems. Lond.
284. *Freibeuter.*
1853. *The Freebooter.* Bowring. Poems. Lond.
285. *Wanderlied.* (Aus *Wilhelm Meister.*)
1824. *Wanderer's Song,* Thos. Carlyle, *Wilhelm Meister.*
Lond., Edin.
1839. *Wanderer's Song,* Dwight. Poems. Bost.
1855. *Wanderer's Song,* R. D. Boylan. *Wilhelm Meister,* Lond.
1856. Same as 1824, *Blackwood's Mag.* LXXX:410.
Edin.
1859. *Wanderer's Song.* Thomas. Poems. Phil.
LOGE
286. *Symbolum.*
1853. *Symbol,* Bowring. Poems. Lond.
287. *Verschwiegenheit.*
1856. (Anon.) *Blackwood's Mag.* LXXX:419. Edin.
GOTT UND WELT
288. *Prooemion.*
1833. One stanza, Mrs. Sarah Austin. *Characteristics of Goethe.* II: 198. Lond.
1839. *Prooemium,* Dwight. Poems. Bost.
1839. Same version, *Western Messenger.* VI: 259.
Louisville.
1853. *Prooemion,* Bowring. Poems. Lond.
289. *Weltseele.*
1839. *World Soul,* Dwight. Poems. Bost.
Dauer im Wechsel
See no. 86.
290. *Eins und Alles.*
1839. *One and All,* Dwight. Poems. Bost.
1839. Same version, *N. Amer. Rev.* XLVIII:510. Bost.
1839. *One and All,* Margaret Fuller. Not published.
291. *Vermächtnis.*
1839. *Our Inheritance,* Dwight. Poems.

Bost.
292. *Parabase.*
1839. *Parabasis,* Dwight. Poems. Bost.
Die Metamorphose der Pflanzen.
See No. 139.
293. *EpirrJiema.*
1839. *Epirrhema,* Dwight. Poems. Bost.
1839. Same version, *Western Messenger.* VII: 14.
Louisville.
294. *Schillers Reliquien.*
1853. *Lines on seeing Schiller's Skull.* Bowring.
Poems. Lond.
"Braun, F. A., *Margaret Fuller and Goethe,* pp. 216-241, Holt & Co., N. T., 1910.
295. *Urworte. Orphisch.*
1837. *Orphic Sayings,* (8) J. F. Clarke, *Western Messenger.* II: 59. Louisville.
1839. Same version, in Dwight's Poems. Bost.
1844. *Primeval Words,* F. H. Hedge. *Christian Examiner.* XXXVII: 247. Bost.
296. *Allerdings. Dem Physiker.*
1839. *By all means, To a Naturalist,* Dwight. Poems. Bost.
297. *Ultimatum.*
1839. *Ultimatum,* Dwight. Poems. Bost.
KDNST
298. *Kunstlerlied.* (Aus den *Wanderjahren.*)
1823. *Artist's Song,* Thos. Carlyle. *Wilhelm Meister.*
Lond., Edin.
1836. *Artist's Song,* J. J. Campbell. *Song of the Bell,* etc. Lond.
1839. *Artist's Song,* Dwight. Poems. Bost.
1855. *Artist's Song,* R. D. Boylan. *Wilhelm Meister.*
Lond.
299. *Ideale.*
1859. *Ideal,* Thomas. Poems. Phil.
300. *Landlich.*
1827. *Unchangedbleness in Love,* C. Des Voeux. *Tasso,* etc. Lond.
301. *Erinnere ich mich doch spat und friih.*
1859. *Pardonable,* Thomas. Poems.

Phil.
EPIGKAMMATISCH
302. *Kronos als Kunstrichter.*
1839. *Time as Epicure,* Dwight. Poems. Bost.
303. *Heut' und evoig.*
1839. *Today and Ever,* Dwight. Poems. Bost.
304. *Lauf der Welt.*
1839. *Written at the Age of 77,* Dwight. Poems. Bost.
1853. *When I was still a youthful Wight,* Bowring. Poems. Lond.
305. *Der Narr epilogiert.*
1839. *The Fool Epilogizes,* Dwight. Poems. Bost.
1853. *The Fool's Epilog,* Bowring. Poems. Lond.
PARABOLISCH
306. *Gedichte sind gemalte Fensterscheiben.*
1839. *Parables,* Dwight. Poems. Bost.
1853. *Song,* Bowring. Poems. Lond.
1859. *Churchivmdow,* Aytoun-Martin. Poems. Lond.
N. Y.
1859. *Poems,* Thomas. Poems. Phil.
307. *Gott sandte seinen rohen Kindern.*
1839. *Poetry,* Dwight. Poems. Bost.
1853. *Poetry,* Bowring. Poems. Lond.
1859. *Poesy,* Aytoun-Martin. Poems. Lond., N. Y.
1859 *Poesy,* Thomas. Poems. Phil.
308. *Zu Regenschauer und Hagelschlag.*
1853. *Should e'er the loveless day,* Bowring. Poems. Lond.
309. *Den Musen-Schwestern fiel es ein.*
1839. *The sister Nine did once propose,* Dwight. Poems. Bost.
1853. *Muses' Plan,* Bowring. Poems. Lond.
1859. *Psyche,* Aytoun-Martin. Poems. Lond., N. Y.
1859. *Cupid and Psyche,* Thomas. Poems. Phil.
310. *Sie saugt mit Gier verrdtrisches Getranke.*
1853. *The Death of the Fly,* Bowring. Poems. Lond.
311. *Wenn du am breiten Flusse wohnst.*
1853. *By the River,* Bowring. Poems.

Lond.

312. *Zwei Personen ganz verschieden.*
1853. *The Fox and the Crane,* Bowring. Poems. Lond.

313. *Schwer, in Waides Busch und Wuchse.*
1853. *The Fox and the Huntsman,* Bowring. Poems. Lond.

314. *Fin grosser Teich war zugefroren.*
1853. *The Frogs,* Bowring. Poems. Lond.
1859. *The Frogs,* Thomas. Poems. Phil.

315. *Im Dorfe war ein gross Gelag.*
1853. *The Wedding,* Bowring. Poems. Lond.
1859. *Wedding Feast,* Aytoun-Martin. Poems. Lond., N. Y.

316. *Ein Magdlein trug man zur Tur hinaus.*
1853. *Burial,* Bowring. Poems. Lond.

317. *Tritt in recht vollem klaren Schein.*
1853. *Threatening Signs,* Bowring. Poems. Lond.

318. *Zu der Apfelverkauferin.*
1853. *The Buyers,* Bowring. Poems. Lond.
1859. *The Buyers,* Thomas. Poems. Phil.

319. *Jetzt war das Bergdorf abgebrannt.*
1853. *The Mountain Village,* Bowring. Poems. Lond.

320. *Im Vatican bedient man sich.*
1853. *Symbols,* Bowring. Poems. Lond.

321. *Drei Palinodien.*
1853. *Three Palinodias,* Bowring. Poems. Lond.

322. *Valet.*
1853. *Valediction,* Bowring. Poems. Lond.

AUS FREMDEN SPEACHEN
323. *Klaggesang. Irisch.*
1836. *An Irish Lamentation,* (J. C. Mangan.) *Dub. Univ. Mag.* VII: 294.
1845. Same version. Mangan's *Anthology.* Dublin.
Zahvt-Xenien
324. *Zahme Xenien.*
1839. *From the "Zahme Xenien"* (12 numbers),
Dwight. Poems. Bost.
1853. *Tame Xenia* (5 numbers),

Bowring. Poems.
Lond.
1856. Anon. *Blackivood's Mag.* LXXX:409. Edin.
(Wenn im Unendlichen.)
(VOL. IV) AUS DEM NACHL.ASS
VERMISCHTE GEDICHTE
325. *Wahrer Genuss.*
1828. *Pleasure,* R. Robinson. Specimens, etc. Lond.
1841. *Felicity,* J. K. Armstrong. *Democratic Bev.* XIX: 356. N. Y.
1853. *True Enjoyment,* Bowring. Poems. Lond.
326. *Ihr verbliihet, siisse Rosen.*
1846. *Despair,* J. Gostwick. *Ger. Lit.* Lond.
1859. *Depression,* Aytomi-Martin. Poems. Lond., N. Y.
1859. *Sadness,* Thomas. Poems. Phil.
327. *Du machst die Alien jung, die Jungen alt.*
1859. *To the New Year,* Thomas. Poems. Phil.
328. *Es war ein fattier Schafer.*
1859. *The Shepherd,* Thomas. Poems. Phil.
329. *Um Mitternacht, wenn die Menschen erst schlafen.*
1859. *A Midnight Fairy Song,* Thomas. Poems. Phil.
330. *Der Brdutigam.*
1853. *The Bridegroom,* Bowring. Poems. Lond.
331. *Dem aufgehenden VoUmonde.*
1853. *To the Rising Full Moon,* Bowring. Poems. Lond.
ANTIKEE FORM SICH NAEHERND
332. *Will ich die Blumen des friihen.*
1853. *Sahontala,* Bowring. Poems. Lond.
PARABOLISCH UND EPIGRAMMATISCH
333. *Beruf des Storches.*
1853. *The Stork's Vocation,* Bowring. Poems. Lond.
334. *Ein Gleichnis.*
1838. *On hearing my songs being translated into Eng-* lish, J. Macray. *Dublin Univ. Mag.* XIII: 642.
335. *Das Schreien.*
1853. *Different Threats,* Bowring. Poems. Lond.
1859. *Two Threats,* Thomas. Poems.

Phil.
336. *Wunsch eines jungen Madchens.*
1853. *Maiden Wishes,* (Anon.) *New Quart. Rev.* II:295. Lond.
1853. *Maiden Wishes,* Bowring. Poems. Lond.
1859. *Girlish Wishes,* Thomas. Poems. Phil.
337. *Liebe und Tugend.*
1853. *Motives,* Bowring. Poems. Lond.
1859. *Motives,* Thomas. Poems. Phil.
338. *Der Misanthrop.*
1853. *The Misanthrope,* Bowring. Poems. Lond.
339. *Zu den Leiden des jungen Werthers.*
1853. *From the Sorrows of Young Werther,* Bowring. Poems. Lond.
340. *Nach dem Italienischen.*
1853. *Paulo post futuri,* Bowring. Poems. Lond.
341. *Hans Liederlich und der Kamerade.*
1853. *Rollicking Hans,* Bowring. Poems. Lond.
AN PERSONEN
342. *Drei Oden an meinen Freund Behrisch.*
1853. *Three Odes to my Friend,* Bowring. Poems. Lond.
343. *Pilgers Morgenlied. An Lila.*
1859. *Pilgrim's Morning Song,* Thomas. Poems. Phil.
344. *An Lili.*
1859. *To Lili,* Thomas. Poems. Phil.
345. *An Frau von Stein. Den 29. Juni 1776.*
1859. *Here Tracing Nature in Repose.* Thomas. Poems. Phil.
UEBERSETZUNGEN
346. *Altschottisch.*
1859. *Goodman and Ooodwife,* Thomas. Poems. Phil.
GOETHE ZUGESCHRIEBENE GEDICHTE ZWEIFELHAFTEN URSPRUNGS
347. *Neun Gedichte an Friederike Brion.*
1859. Thomas. Poems. Phil. (Contains eight of the nine poems, omitting no. 7, *Balde seh' ich Riekchen wieder.)*

348. *Madchens Held.*
1853. *Such, such is he,* Bowring.
Poems. Lond.
(VOL. V) AUS DEM NACHLASS
VERMISCHTE GEDICHTE
349. *Nacht, o holde! halbes Leben.*
1859. *Night,* Thomas. Poems. Phil.
350. *Ein Schauspiel fur Gotter.*
1847. *The Happy Pair,* Anon. *Amer.
Whig Mag.*
V:122. N. Y.
351. *Es rauschet das Wasser.*
1856. *Unchanging,* Anon. *Blackwood's
Mag.* LXXX:
419. Edin.
352. *Aus WiUielm Meister.* (Neun
kleinere Gedichte.)
1824. Thos. Carlyle. *Wilhelm Meister.*
Lond. Edin.
1855. E. D. Boylan, *Wilhelm Meister.*
Lond.
1859. Thomas. Poems. Phil.
See also no. 198.
353. *Die Zerstdrung Magdeburgs.*
1853. *The Destruction of Magdeburg.*
Bowring. Poems.
Lond.
ZAHME XENIEN
354. *Gut verloren—etwas verloren.*
1839. *Goods gone—something gone,*
Dwight. Poems.
Bost.
1853. *// wealth is gone,* Bowring.
Poems. Lond.
355. *Wittst du dir ein hubsch Leben zim-
mern.*
1839. *Rule of Life* (Enlarged) Dwight.
Poems. Bost.
1853. *Rule of Life,* Bowring. Poems.
Lond.
356. *Angedenken.*
1853. *Remembrance of the Good,*
Bowring. Poems.
Lond.
357. *Den Vereinigten Staaten.*
1830. *To the United States,* Anon. *Edin.
Lit. Journal.*
IV: 258.
1831. *To the United States,* Same version, *Fraser's
Mag.* III: 452. Lond.
1834. *To the United States,* Anon. *Lond.
Mo. Mag.*
XXXIV-.52.
1834. *To the United States,* Same ver-

sion, *Atkinson's
Casket.* IX: 36. Phil.
(VOL. Vi) WEST-OESTLICHER DIVAN
358. *West-östlicher Divan.*
1837. Bettina von Arnim. *Goethe's Cor-
respondence
with a Child.* Lond. (1840, Bost.)
*Haben sie von deinen Fehlen; Als ich
auf dem
Euphrat; Dies zu deuten; Wie mit innig-
stem
Beilagen.*
1853. Bowring. Poems. Lond.
*Talismane; Vier Gnaden; Zwiespalt;
Lied und
Gebilde.—Unbegrenzt.—Musterbilder;
Noch ein
Paar; Eine Stelle suchte.—Fiinf Dinge;
Be-
handelt die Frauen; Ferdusi spricht;
Suleika
spricht.—Sich selbst zu loben.—22
"Sprüche."
—Der Winter und Timur; An Suleika.—
Dass
Suleika von Jussuph; Nicht Gelegen-
heit; Die
Sonne kommt; Lieb' um Liebe; Locken
haltet
mich; An vollen Büschelzweigen; Was
bedeutet;
Hochbild; Ach, um deine; Wiederfind-
en; Wie
mit innigstem Behagen; In tausend For-
men.—
Ob der Koran; Sie haben wegen.—Vom
Him-
mel sank; Bulbuls Nachtlied; Ich sah
mit
Staunen; Alle Menschen; Es ist gut.—
Ver-
mächtnis.—Berechtigte   Männer;
Begünstigte,
Tiere; Siebenschläfer. Aus dem Nachlass:
Hafis, dir sich; Sprich, unter; Und
warum
sendet; Schreibt er in Neski.*
Goedeke's *Grundriss* mentions (p. 497,
§242) translations of parts of the *Divan*
as given in *Blackwood's Mag.* XI: 68,
1859. This article does not however
contain any translations from Goethe,
but rather it is a review of RUxert's
(Rückert's?) *Oestliche Bosen,* with a

poetical dedication to Goethe in the
style of Goethe's *Divan.*
The present edition of Bowring's translations of *Goethe's Poems* as published
by Bell & Co., Lond., in the *Bohn Standard Library,* contains a translation of
the entire *Divan;* this, however, was not
done until 1874.
The edition of 1853 contained the translation of about sixty various poems
from the *Divan.* Aside from those, only
the very few scattered translations,
mentioned above, could be found previous to 1860, in fact practically nothing
that gave in any way an idea of the nature of the collection.
1859. Aytoun-Martin. Poems. Lond., N.
T.
Siebenschlafer.
1859. Thomas. Poems. Phil.
*Das Leben ist ein Gansespiel; Ach um
deine
feuchten Schwingen; Deinem Blick
mich zu be-
quemen; Nicht Gelegenheit macht
Diebe.*
(VOL. XVI) VERMISCHTE GEDICHTE
359. *Parabeln.* (Ein Meister einer
landlichen Schule.)
1853. *The Country Schoolmaster,*
Bowring. Poems.
    Lond.
360. *Legende vom Hufeisen.*
1850. *The Horseshoe,* C. R. Lambert.
Poems, etc. Lond.
1853. *The Legend of the Horseshoe,*
Bowring. Poems.
Lond.
1859. *St. Peter and the Cherries,* Aytoun-Martin.
Poems. Lond., N. Y.
1859. *The Legend of the Horseshoe,*
Thomas. Poems.
    Phil.
361. *Hans Sachsens poetische Sendung.*
1853. *Hans Sachs' Poetical Mission,*
Bowring. Poems.
Lond.
362. *Auf Miedings Tod.*
1833. *Mieding's Death,* 46 lines, Mrs.
Sarah Austin.
Goethe's Characteristics. I:156. Lond.
363. *Epilog zu Schillers Glocke.*
1835. *Epilogue to Schiller's Bell,* (J. C.
Mangan) *Dub.*

Univ. Mag. V: 57.

1839. *In Memory of Schiller,* J. F. Clark,
in Dwight's
  Poems. Bost.

1853. *Epilogue to Schiller's Bell,*
Bowring. Poems.
Lond.

1859. *Epilogue to Schiller's Bell,* Aytoun-Martin.
Poems. Lond., N. Y.

364. *Die HoUenfahrt Jesu Christi.*

1853. *Thoughts on Jesus Christ's Des-
cent into Hell,*
Bowring. Poems. Lond.

(VOL. Vm) AUS EGMONT

365. *Clarchens Lied.* (Freudvoll und lei-
dvoll.)

1835. *Clarchen's Song,* L. E. L(andon)
Lit. Gazette.
p. 138. Lond.

1842. *Clarchen's Song,* J. A. A(nster).
Dub. Univ.
Mag. XX: 615.

1848. *Clarchen's Song,* Anon. *North
British Rev.*

1848. *Clarchen's Song,* same version,
Eclectic Mag.
p. 15. N.Y.

1852. *Clara's Song,* Mrs. Haller. Translations, etc.
  Lond.

1853. *Clara's Song,* Bowring. Poems.
Lond.

1856. *Clara's Song,* (Anon.) *National
Rev.* II: 18.
Lond.

1856. *Clara's Song,* same version, *LitteU's Living Age.*
L:25. Bost.

366. *Die Trommel geruhret!*

1829. *Clara's Song,* Zarach. *Pocket
Mag.* p. 40. Lond.

1853. *Clara's Song,* Bowring. Poems.
Lond.

(vol. X) Iphigente

367. *Opening Monologue.*

1827. C. Des Voeux. *Tasso* etc. Lond.

1837. Bettina von Arnim. *Goethe's Correspondence
with a Child.* Lond.

"Aside from these scattered translations, there were six complete translations of *Egmont* before 1860. See
Oswald, E., *Goethe m England
and America,* 2. edition, Lond., 1909, p.

19.

"Previous to 1860, there were six complete translations of the 7pM-
genia. None of those are included here.
I have given only scattered translations
of the distinctly lyrical portions.
Oswald, E., in his bibliography, *Goethe
in England and America,* pp.
50—51, gives five complete translations. To these should be added a sixth,
Metrical Translation of Iphigenia, by
Judge Beverly Tucker, in *The Southern Lit. Messenger,* X: 2, 65, 129, 265:
1844.

3G8. *Song of the Fates.*

1830. *Song of the Fates,* Wm. Taylor.
*Hist. Survey of
Ger. Poetry.* Lond.

1832. *Song of the Fates,* F. H. *New Mo.
Mag.*
XXXIV: 407. Lond.

1839. *Song of the Fates,* N. L. Frothingham in
Dwight's Poems. Bost.

1839. *Selections,* Mrs. Hemans, *New
Mo. Mag.* XL: 1-8.

1844. Same as 1830, *Dub. Univ. Mag.*
XXIII: 312.

1852. *Song of the Fates,* Mrs. Haller.
Translations.
  Lond.

1853. *Song of the Fates,* Bowring.
Poems. Lond.

1855. Same as 1839, Frothingham. *Metrical Versions
from the German.* Bost.

1859. *Song of the Fates,* Margaret
Fuller Ossoli. *Life
Without and Within.* Bost.

(VOL. Xn) DIE FISCHERIN

369. *Es war ein Bitter.*

1845. *Cavalier's Choice,* (Aytoun.)
Blackwood's Mag.
LVII:174. Edin.

1859. Same version, Aytoun-Martin.
Poems. London,
N. Y.

370. *0. Mutter,, guten Bat.*

1795. *The Water King,* M. G. Lewis.
The Monk. Lond.

1801. Same version, M. G. Lewis. *Tales
of Wonder.*
Lond.

1834. *The Water Sprite,* T. J. A. *Tait's
Edin. Mag.*

I:520.

1845. *The Waterman,* (Martin.) *Blackwood's Mag.*
LVII:165. Edin.

1859. Same version, Aytoun-Martin.
Poems. London,
  N. Y.

This poem was used by Goethe In *Die
Fischerin* and was ascribed by early
translators to him. It is really of Danish
origin and was first published in 1779,
in Herder's *Tolksliedern, TV,* 13 as *Der
Wassermann.*

(VOL. XT?) FAUST

371. *Zueignung.*

1820. *Dedication to Faust,* (J. Anster.)
*Dub. Univ.
Mag.* VII: 236.

1835. *Dedication to Faust,* J. G. Fliigel.
*Flowers of
German Poetry.* Lond.

1836. *Dedication to Faust,* J. J. Campbell. *Song of
the BeU.* Lond.

1839. *Inscription to Faust,* Dwight.
Poems. Bost.

1845. *Dedication to Faust,* G. F. Duckett. *Translations
from Faust.* Lond.

1845. *Dedication to Faust,* A. H.
Everett. Poems. Bost.

1845. *Dedication to Faust,* F. G. Halleck in Longfellow's *Poets of Europe.*
Phil.

1850. *Dedication to Faust,* "P". *Amer.
Whig Rev.*
XII: 470. N. Y.

1852. *Dedication to Faust,* Mrs. A.
Haller. Transla-
tions, etc, Lond.

1853. *Dedication to Faust,* Bowring.
Poems. Lond.

1859. *Dedication to Faust,* Nominis
Umbra, *TJie Roman
Martyr.* Lond.

372. *Prolog im Himmel.*

1824. *Prologue in Heaven,* Percy
Bysshe Shelley.
Posthumous Works. Lond.

1826. Same version, *L. Quart. Rev.*
XXXIV: 136.

1835. *Song of the Archangels,* Anon.
South. Lit. Jour.
  I:53. Charleston, S. C.

1836. *Song of the Angels,* J. Anster.

Dub. Univ. Mag.
VII: 282.

"Previous to 1860, there were at least eighteen translations of the entire first part of *Faust,* and seven of the second part. In my above list I have not included any of these versions, except when they occurred apart from the complete text, in anthologies, essays, or magazines, where they have oftentimes been used and the authorship not mentioned. For lists of the various translations of Faust see Oswald, E., *Qoethe in England and America,* 2. edition, Lond. , 1909; Hauhart, W. H., *Goethe's Faust in England and America,* Columbia Univ. Press, N. T., 1909; Baumann, Lina, *Die englischen Uebersetzungen von Goethes Faust,* Halle. 1907.

1836. *Song of the Angels,* J. Blackie. *Dub. Univ. Mag.*
VII: 282.

1836. *Song of the Angels,* F. Egerton. *Dub. Univ. Mag.*
VII: 283.

1836. *Song of the Angels,* (Mangan.) *Dub. Univ. Mag.*
VII: 283.

1839. *Song of the Angels,* G. W. Haven in Dwight's
Poems. Bost.

1839. Same version, *Western Messenger.* VI: 259.
Louisville, Ky.

1839. *Prolog in Heaven,* S. Naylor. A Drama etc.
  Maidenhead, Eng.

1840. *Chorus of Angels,* J. E. Reade. *The Drama of Life.* Lond.

1841. Same as 1839, Haven. *Ladies' Repository.* I:127.
  Cincinnati, O.

1842. Same as 1839, Haven. *New Hampshire Book.*
  Bost.

1842. *Prolog in Heaven,* Algernon. *Ideals.* Phil.

1844. *Song of Angels.* J. H. Merivale. Poems Orig.
and Trans. Lond.

1845. *Prolog in Heaven,* G. F. Duckett. *Translations from Faust.* Lond.

1845. *Prolog in Heaven,* J. Gostwick. *Spirit of German Poetry.* Lond.

1846. *Prolog in Heaven,* Capt. Knox. *Oxford and Camb. Rev.* II:207.

1849. *Song of Angels,* C. T. Brooks. *Lit. World.* V: 349.
  N. T.

1850. *Chorus of Angels,* F. H. Hedge in Furness' *Song of the Bell.* Phil.

1850. *Hymn of the Angels,* C. R. Lambert. *Poems.* Lond.

1853. *Chorus of Angels,* Bowring. Poems. Lond.

1853. Same as 1850, Hedge in *Furness' Gems of Ger. Verse.* Phil.
Goedeke's *Grundrlss* states that 6 poems are to be found here translated; as a matter of fact only the *Prolog* is to be found.

1857. Same as 1824, Shelley. *V. S. Mag.* IV: 86. N. Y., Washington.

1859. *Song of the Archangels,* Thomas. Poems. Phil.

373. *Fausts Monolog.*
1820. (J.Anster.) *Blackwood's Mag.* VII: 237. Edin.

1822 Lines 1-576. George Soames. Boosey, Lond.

1826. *Youth,* F. L. Gower. *L. Quart. Rev.* XXXIV: 137.

1827. C. Des Voeux. *Tasso* etc. Lond.

1828. *Youth,* Anon. *Athenaeum.* No. 59, I:939. Lond.
(With imitation by Thos. Moore.)

1836. *Monologue,* Chas. Hodges. *Faust Scenes.* Lond

1842. *Monologue,* Anon. *Magnolia.* TV: 42. Savannah.

374. *Der Schafer schmiickte sich zum Tanz.*
1820. *The Shepherd for the Dance was Dressed,* (J. Anster.) *Blackwood's Mag.* VII: 244. Edin.

1859. *The Shepherd for the Dance was Dressed,*
  Thomas. Poems. Phil.

375. *Der Osterspaziergang.*

1820. (J.Anster.) *Blackwood's Mag.* VII: 243. Edin.

1826. *The Easter Walk,* F. L. Gower. *L. Quart. Rev.* XXXIV: 141.

1828. *The Easter Walk,* F. Page. *Employment.* Bath, Eng.

1831. *The Easter Walk,* Anon. *Edin. Lit. Journal.*
  V:187.

1840. *The Easter Walk,* R. Talbot. *Dub. Univ. Mag.* IX: 498.

1845. *The Easter Walk,* A. H. Everett Poems. Bost.

1853. *The Easter Walk,* Anon. *N. Y. Quarterly.* I: 416.

376. *Der Fluch.*
1820. *The Curse,* (J. Anster.) *Blackwood's Mag.* VII: 248. Edin.

1832. *The Curse,* Thos. Carlyle. *Athenaeum,* no. 219, p. 5. Lond.

377. *Wald und Hbhle.*
1813. *Wood and Cavern,* Mme. de Stael. *Germany.* Lond., Bosk, N. Y., Phil.

1820. *Faust's Soliloquy.* (J. Anster.) *Blackwood's Magazine.* VII: 255. Edin.

1834. *Faust's Soliloquy,* P. B. *New Eng. Mag.* VII: 365. Boat.

1836. *Forest and Cave,* Chas. Hodges. *Faust* Scenes.
  Lond.

1840. *Forest and Cavern,* J. E. Reade. *The Drama of Life.* Lond.

1855. *Wood and Cavern,* J. Blackie, in Lewes' *Life of Goethe.* Lond., Bost.

378. *Meine Ruh' ist hin.*
1820. *My Peace is Gone,* (J. Anster.) *Blackwood's Mag.* VII: 256. Edin.

1821. *My Peace of Mind's Ruined,* (G. Soane?) *European Mag.* LXXX: 366. Lond.

1836. *My Peace is Vanished,,* F. Egerton Leveson Gower.
Dub. Univ. Mag. VII: 288.

1836. *My Rest is Gone,* J. S. Blackie.

Dub. Univ.

Mag. VII: 288.

1836. *My Peace is Departed,* (Mangan.
) *Dub. Univ.*

Mag. VII: 289.

1836. Same as 1820, Anster. *Dub. Univ.*

Mag. VII: 288.

1839. *My Peace is Hence,* G. W. Haven,
in Dwight's

Poems. Bost.

1845. *My Heart is Heavy,* L. Fillmore in
Gostwick's

Spirit of Ger. Poetry. Lond.

1846. *I am Wearying,* E. Helfenstein.
Godey's Lady's

Book. XXXII: 193. Phil.

1852. *My Heart is Oppressed,* Mrs.
Haller. Transla-

tions, etc. Lond.

1853. *My Heart is Sad,* Bowring.
Poems. Lond.

1858. *My Peace is Gone,* G. Turner.
Train. V:300.

Lond.

1859. *My Peace is Gone,* Thomas.
Poems. Phil.

"The same version is used in *Masterpieces of the World's Best Literature,* edited by Jeannette Guilder, IV:
178, 1910.

379. *Ach neige, du Schmerzenreiche.*

1840. *Mater Dolorosa,* J. E. Reade. *The
Drama of Life.*

381. *Walpurgisnacht.*

1822. *Mayday Night,* Percy Bysshe
Shelley. *The Lib-
eral.* I:120. Lond.

1824. *Mayday Night,* Shelley's *Posthumous Poems.*

Lond.

1824. Same version, *Edin. Rev.* XL: 510.

1826. Same version, *L. Quarterly Rev.*
XXXIV: 149.

1830. Same version, in Taylor's *Hist.
Survey of Ger.
Poetry.* Lond.

1839. *The Walpurgis Night,* J. E. Reade.
*L. Mo.
Chronical.* IV: 405.

1840. Same version, Reade's *The Drama of Life.* Lond.

1845. Same as 1822, in Longfellow's
Poets of Europe.

Lond., Phil.

382. *Marthens Garten. Fausts*

Glaubensbekenntnis.

1813. *Faust's Confession of Faith,*
Mme. de Stael.

Germany. Lond., Bost., N. Y., Phil.

1832. *Dialog of Faust and Marguerite,*
Henry Crabb

Eobinson. *Monthly Repository.* VI:
756.

1833. *Faust and Marguerite,* Mrs. S.
Austin. *Goethe's
Characteristics.* I:279. Lond., N. Y.

383. *Kerker.*

1813. *Prison Scene,* Mme. de Stael.
Germany. Lond.,

Bost., N. Y., Phil.

1820. *Prison Scene,* (J. Anster.) *Blackwood's Mag.*

VII: 257. Edin.

1836. *In Prison,* Chas. Hodges. *Faust
Scenes.* Lond.

384. *Scattered translations from the
second part of Faust.*

1828. *Helena,* Thos. Carlyle. *Foreign
Rev.* I:429.

Lond. (Also found in the editions of
his essays.)

1836. *Dirge over Euphorion,* J. F.
Clark. *West. Mes-
senger.* I:474.

1845. *Opening Scene,* J. Gostwick.
*Spirit of Ger.
Poetry.* Lond.

1853. *Opening Scene,* Bowring. Poems.
Lond.

1853. *Angels' Chorus,* in the last scene,
Bowring. Poems.
Lond.

1853. *Scene at the Court of the Emper-
or,* Sarah Whitman. *Hours of Life.* Providence, K. I.

1858. *Helena,* Martin. *Fraser's Mag.*
LVTI:63. Lond.

F.—List Of Translators And Poems
Translated By Each

Algernon. 23, 372, 384.

A ("M. M. A.") 104, 105, 108, 109,
110.

Anster, John. 126, 128, 165, 365,
371, 372, 373, 374, 375, 376, 377, 378,
379, 383. Armstrong, J. K. 325.

Arnim, Bettina von. 72, 144, 147,
148, 150, 151, 152, 153, 158, 159, 358,
367.

Austin, Mrs. Sarah. 73, 93, 95, 136,
138, 139, 142, 173, 179, 288, 362, 382.

Aytoun and Martin. 1, 4, 6, 9,
10,11,13, 22, 23, 24, 25, 27, 28, 30, 34,
35, 37, 38, 39, 45, 46, 49, 52, 53, 54, 56,
57, 60, 63, 64, 66, 68, 69, 70, 71, 72, 73,
74, 75, 80, 84, 91, 103, 104, 105, 106,
107, 108, 109, 110, 112, 113, 118, 119,
122, 123, 125, 127, 128, 129, 164, 165,
166, 173, 174, 175, 179, 184, 186, 188,
189, 198, 199, 201, 202, 203, 204, 205,
206, 207, 208, 209, 210, 211, 212, 213,
214, 215, 216, 217, 218, 219, 220, 221,
223, 224, 225, 226, 271, 306, 309, 315,
326, 358, 360, 363, 369, 370.

B ("S.E. B.") 20, 39.

Bancroft, George. 6, 41, 69, 103, 105,
108, 110, 164, 167, 172, 176, 226.

Baskerville, Alfred. 6, 9, 10, 13, 14,
45, 46, 49, 50, 52, 60, 63, 64, 75, 85,
103, 104, 105,107, 108, 113, 122, 130.

Benton, Joel. 52, 107.

Beresford, —. 37, 74, 75, 103, 104,
105, 108, 109.

Berkeley, H. 107.

Bernays, L. J. 93, 103.

Blackie, John. 372, 377, 378.

Blackwood's Mag. 49, 50, 52, 60, 62,
68, 70, 71, 72, 73, 93, 102, 103, 105,
107, 108, 109, 110, 113, 125, 127, 128,
129, 131, 142, 164, 173, 189, 198, 199,
201, 202, 203, 204, 205, 206, 207, 208,
209, 210, 211, 212, 213, 214, 215, 217,
218, 219, 220, 221, 225, 226, 234, 285,
287, 324, 351, 369, 370, 373, 374, 375,
376, 377, 378, 383, 384, 385.

Bokum, Hermann. 41.

Boothby, Sir Brooke, 129.

Borrow, George 0. 107.

Bowring, Edgar A. 1, 3, 4, 5, 6, 7, 8,
9, 10, 11, 12, 13, 14,
15, 16, 17, 18, 19, 20, 21, 22, 23, 24, 25,
26, 27, 28, 29,
30, 32, 33, 34, 35, 36, 37, 38, 39, 40, 41,
42, 43, 44, 45,
46, 47, 48, 49, 50, 51, 52, 53, 54, 55, 56,
57, 58, 59, 60,
61, 62, 63, 64, 65, 66, 67, 68, 69, 70, 71,
72, 73, 74, 75,
79, 80, 81, 82, 83, 84, 85, 86, 87, 89, 91,
92, 93, 94, 95,
96, 97, 98, 99, 100, 101, 102, 103, 104,
105, 106, 107, 108,
109, 110, 111, 112, 113, 114, 115, 116,
117, 118, 119, 120,
121, 122, 123, 124, 125, 126, 127, 128,
129, 130, 131, 133,

G.—INDEX OF POEMS

The following alphabetic list of poems found in translation refers to the numbers in Bibliography E. No individual entries have been made for the groups *Gereimte Distichen* (241), *Sprichwdrtlich* (242), and *Zahme Xenien* (324), nor for such passages or scenes from larger works as are not distinct songs or poems.

Lightning Source UK Ltd.
Milton Keynes UK
UKOW04f1900051216

289269UK00010B/352/P